60-SECOND
Refreshment

Power Prayers
for Women

60-SECOND
Refreshment

Power Prayers *for* Women

BARBOUR
PUBLISHING

Compiled by Jill Jones.

ISBN 978-1-64352-763-5

Text edited and compiled from *Power Prayers for Women* by
Jackie M. Johnson. Published by Barbour Publishing, Inc.

Published by Barbour Publishing, 1810 Barbour Drive,
Uhrichsville, Ohio 44683, www.barbourbooks.com

*Our mission is to inspire the world with the life-changing
message of the Bible.*

Member of the
Evangelical Christian
Publishers Association

Printed in China.

WE'RE ALL PRESSED FOR TIME.
BUT SOMEWHERE IN OUR DAILY
SCHEDULE, THERE MUST BE AT
LEAST SIXTY FREE SECONDS.

Look for that open minute and fill it
with this book. *60-Second Refreshment: Power Prayers for Women*
provides quick, inspiring devotional
prayers for every day of the year,
promising real spiritual refreshment and encouragement. Use each
day's prayer as a kick-start for your
own time of conversation with God.

Read on, and find the refreshment your soul craves!

Day 1

Lord, I long to be
more connected to You.
Teach me to worship You as the
true source of power and love.
I adore You like no other.
Transform me so my prayers
will be powerful and my
life will be fruitful.

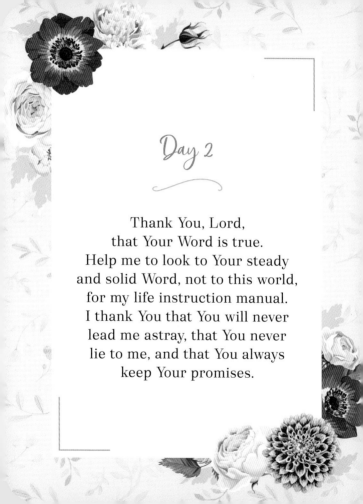

Day 2

Thank You, Lord,
that Your Word is true.
Help me to look to Your steady
and solid Word, not to this world,
for my life instruction manual.
I thank You that You will never
lead me astray, that You never
lie to me, and that You always
keep Your promises.

Day 3

Lord, I want to be equipped
to live life as a Christ follower.
You breathed Your life into the
words that men put on parchment–
which are now the words of the
Bible. Correct and train me
in righteousness so that I will
be ready for whatever
life holds for me.

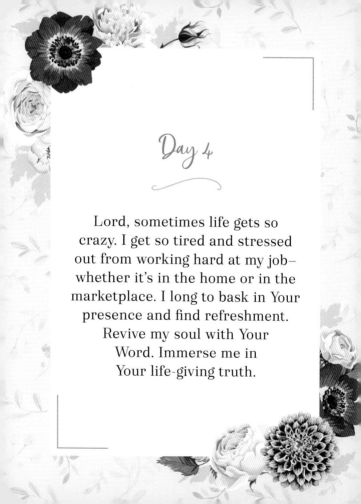

Day 4

Lord, sometimes life gets so crazy. I get so tired and stressed out from working hard at my job—whether it's in the home or in the marketplace. I long to bask in Your presence and find refreshment. Revive my soul with Your Word. Immerse me in Your life-giving truth.

Day 5

Lord, Your words are right and
true; they bring joy to my heart.
I need more joy. Happiness comes
and goes, but joy is deep and
lasting. I need Your true joy despite
my circumstances and feelings.
Your commands illuminate me so
I can live revitalized each day.

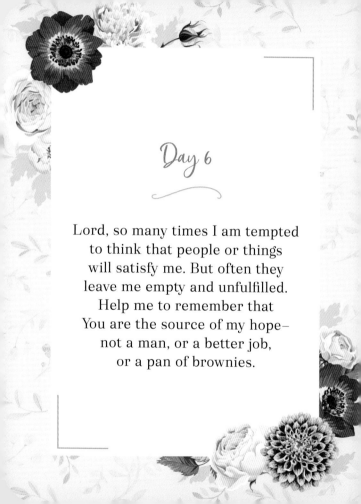

Day 6

Lord, so many times I am tempted
to think that people or things
will satisfy me. But often they
leave me empty and unfulfilled.
Help me to remember that
You are the source of my hope–
not a man, or a better job,
or a pan of brownies.

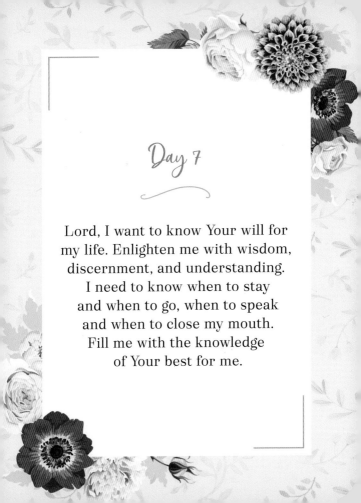

Day 7

Lord, I want to know Your will for
my life. Enlighten me with wisdom,
discernment, and understanding.
I need to know when to stay
and when to go, when to speak
and when to close my mouth.
Fill me with the knowledge
of Your best for me.

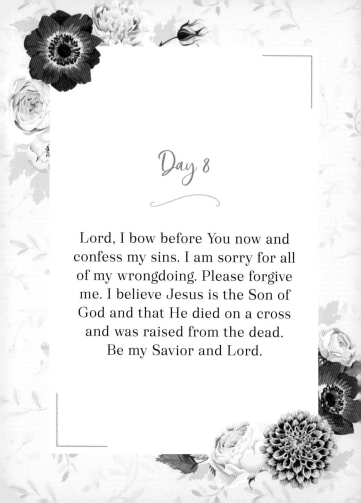

Day 8

Lord, I bow before You now and
confess my sins. I am sorry for all
of my wrongdoing. Please forgive
me. I believe Jesus is the Son of
God and that He died on a cross
and was raised from the dead.
Be my Savior and Lord.

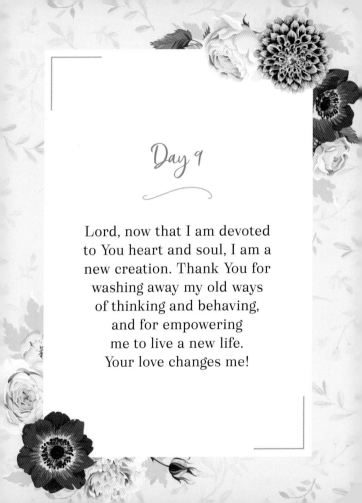

Day 9

Lord, now that I am devoted
to You heart and soul, I am a
new creation. Thank You for
washing away my old ways
of thinking and behaving,
and for empowering
me to live a new life.
Your love changes me!

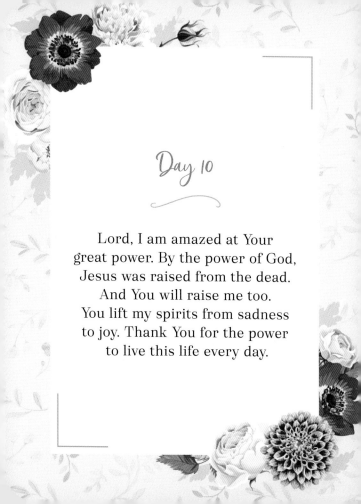

Day 10

Lord, I am amazed at Your
great power. By the power of God,
Jesus was raised from the dead.
And You will raise me too.
You lift my spirits from sadness
to joy. Thank You for the power
to live this life every day.

Day 11

Lord, You know how painful it is
when things are not right between
friends. What a joy it is to know
that I am made right with God by
faith. We can communicate freely,
talking and listening, enjoying each
other as heart friends. Thank You
for restoration and righteousness.

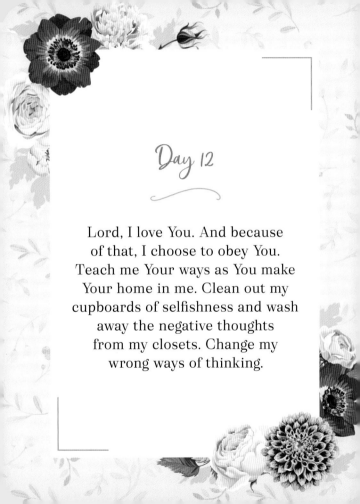

Day 12

Lord, I love You. And because
of that, I choose to obey You.
Teach me Your ways as You make
Your home in me. Clean out my
cupboards of selfishness and wash
away the negative thoughts
from my closets. Change my
wrong ways of thinking.

Day 13

Lord, I am not ashamed of the Gospel. Your words have the power to bring salvation to every person who believes. I don't want to hide the light of truth, but instead I want to let it shine from my life so others will see Christ in me.

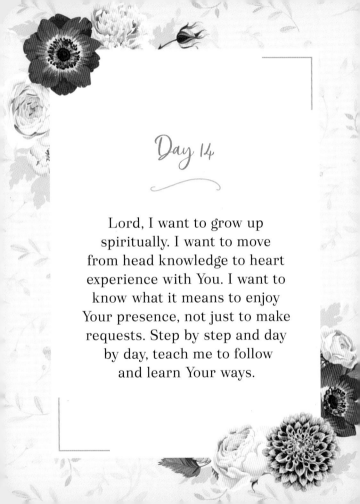

Day 14

Lord, I want to grow up
spiritually. I want to move
from head knowledge to heart
experience with You. I want to
know what it means to enjoy
Your presence, not just to make
requests. Step by step and day
by day, teach me to follow
and learn Your ways.

Day 15

Lord, here I am before You. I am ready to "take up my cross" and follow You. Every day I want to be with You, empowered by You, and loved so deeply that I am changed. Show me what it means to lose my life in order to save it.

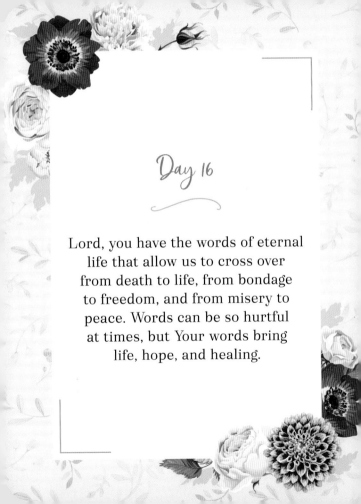

Day 16

Lord, you have the words of eternal
life that allow us to cross over
from death to life, from bondage
to freedom, and from misery to
peace. Words can be so hurtful
at times, but Your words bring
life, hope, and healing.

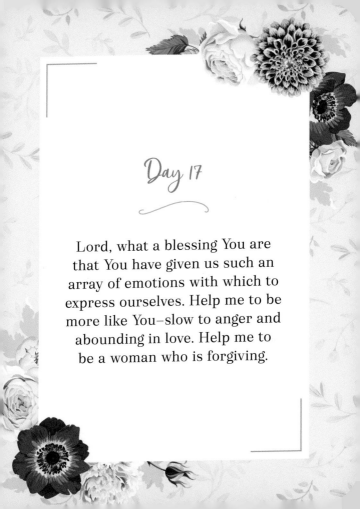

Day 17

Lord, what a blessing You are
that You have given us such an
array of emotions with which to
express ourselves. Help me to be
more like You–slow to anger and
abounding in love. Help me to
be a woman who is forgiving.

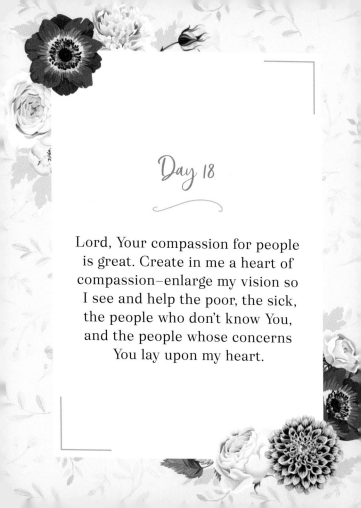

Day 18

Lord, Your compassion for people
is great. Create in me a heart of
compassion–enlarge my vision so
I see and help the poor, the sick,
the people who don't know You,
and the people whose concerns
You lay upon my heart.

Day 19

Lord, I thank You that You are my true companion–that I am never alone. You have assigned angels to watch over and protect me. You have given me Your Holy Spirit and promised that You are with me always, even to the very end of the age.

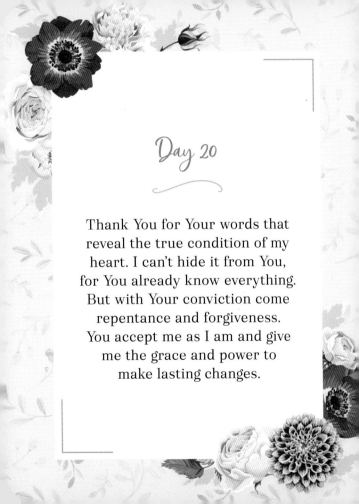

Day 20

Thank You for Your words that
reveal the true condition of my
heart. I can't hide it from You,
for You already know everything.
But with Your conviction come
repentance and forgiveness.
You accept me as I am and give
me the grace and power to
make lasting changes.

Day 21

Lord, I am so angry and I need Your help. I need to do something with this heated emotion—and I choose to give You my anger and bitterness. Help me be rid of it. Redeem the confusion and bring peace to what seems so out of control.

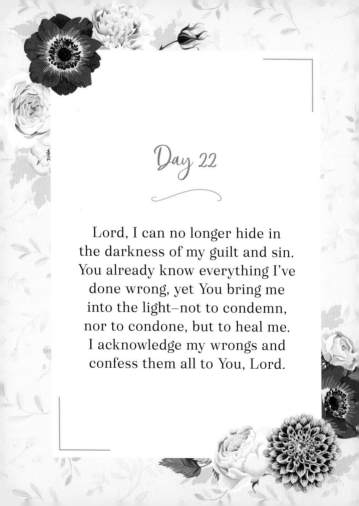

Day 22

Lord, I can no longer hide in the darkness of my guilt and sin. You already know everything I've done wrong, yet You bring me into the light–not to condemn, nor to condone, but to heal me. I acknowledge my wrongs and confess them all to You, Lord.

Day 23

Lord, thank You for Your gift of eternal life and the power to do Your will. I cannot fathom how You suffered, yet You did it all for me— for every person. You bled for my sins. You had victory over death. You made a way for me. Thank You, Lord.

Day 24

Lord, I don't know what to do–but
You certainly do. Lead me on the
right course of action; show me
when to speak and when to be
silent, when to move and when
to be still. Help me to listen
and follow Your ways.

Day 25

Lord, thank You for the joy and
closeness my husband and I share.
When we do something wrong,
help each of us to forgive and move
past the offense. I pray that our
love would be patient and kind,
not proud or selfish but
seeking each other's good.

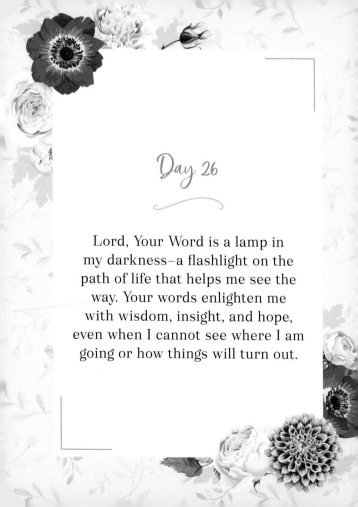

Day 26

Lord, Your Word is a lamp in
my darkness—a flashlight on the
path of life that helps me see the
way. Your words enlighten me
with wisdom, insight, and hope,
even when I cannot see where I am
going or how things will turn out.

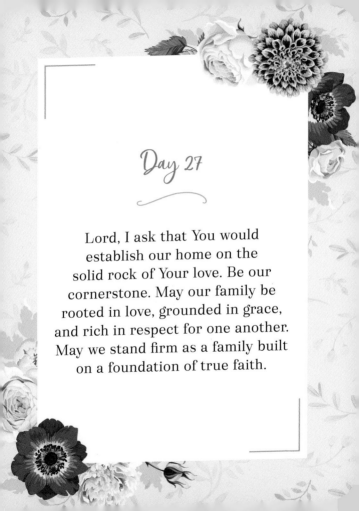

Day 27

Lord, I ask that You would
establish our home on the
solid rock of Your love. Be our
cornerstone. May our family be
rooted in love, grounded in grace,
and rich in respect for one another.
May we stand firm as a family built
on a foundation of true faith.

Day 28

Lord, be our strong defense and protect our home. May this be a place of safety, comfort, and peace. Guard us from outside forces and protect us from harmful attacks from within. I pray that the Holy Spirit would put a hedge of protection around our home and family.

Day 29

Lord, thank You for my good
health. I pray for Your power
to sustain me as I take care of
myself—by eating healthy food,
drinking enough water, and making
movement and exercise a part
of my daily life. Please keep
me from injury and illness.

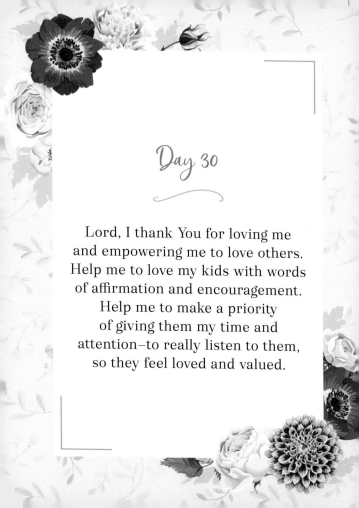

Day 30

Lord, I thank You for loving me
and empowering me to love others.
Help me to love my kids with words
of affirmation and encouragement.
Help me to make a priority
of giving them my time and
attention—to really listen to them,
so they feel loved and valued.

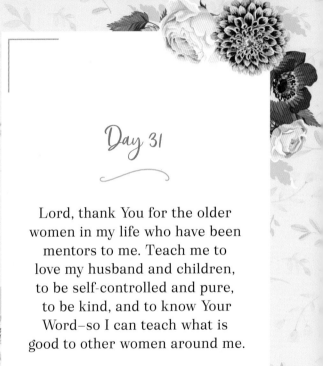

Day 31

Lord, thank You for the older
women in my life who have been
mentors to me. Teach me to
love my husband and children,
to be self-controlled and pure,
to be kind, and to know Your
Word–so I can teach what is
good to other women around me.

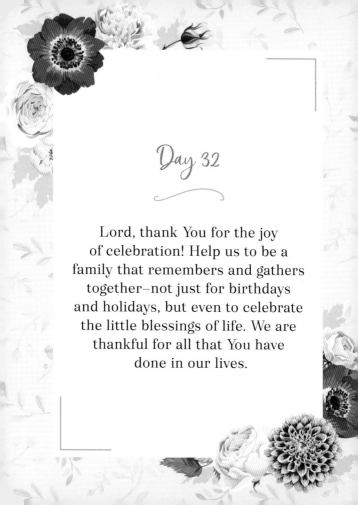

Day 32

Lord, thank You for the joy of celebration! Help us to be a family that remembers and gathers together—not just for birthdays and holidays, but even to celebrate the little blessings of life. We are thankful for all that You have done in our lives.

Day 33

Lord, bless this new house.
We dedicate it to You. Bring protection
to this place. Fill each room with
Your loving presence, Your peace,
and Your power. May we treat each
other with respect and guests
with warmth. Use this house to
bring glory to Your name.

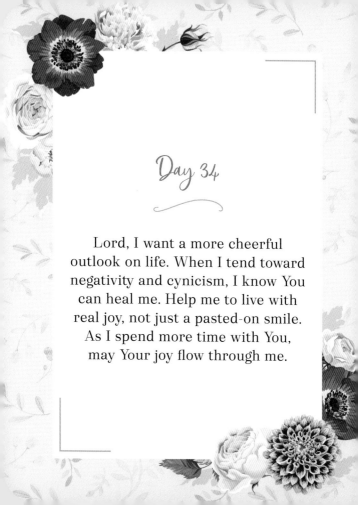

Day 34

Lord, I want a more cheerful outlook on life. When I tend toward negativity and cynicism, I know You can heal me. Help me to live with real joy, not just a pasted-on smile. As I spend more time with You, may Your joy flow through me.

Day 35

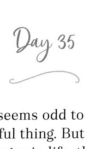

Lord, it seems odd to consider
trials a joyful thing. But I pray that
my challenges in life, these times
of testing, will lead me to
greater perseverance. May that
perseverance finish its work
so I will be mature and complete,
on my way to wholeness.

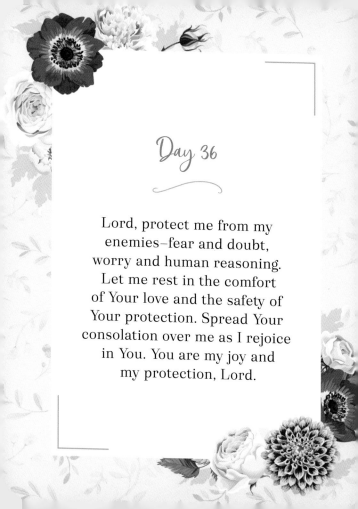

Day 36

Lord, protect me from my
enemies–fear and doubt,
worry and human reasoning.
Let me rest in the comfort
of Your love and the safety of
Your protection. Spread Your
consolation over me as I rejoice
in You. You are my joy and
my protection, Lord.

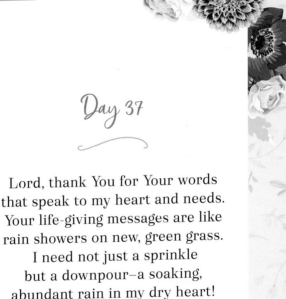

Day 37

Lord, thank You for Your words
that speak to my heart and needs.
Your life-giving messages are like
rain showers on new, green grass.
I need not just a sprinkle
but a downpour—a soaking,
abundant rain in my dry heart!

Day 38

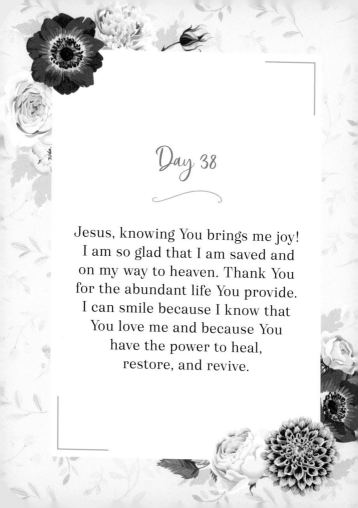

Jesus, knowing You brings me joy!
I am so glad that I am saved and
on my way to heaven. Thank You
for the abundant life You provide.
I can smile because I know that
You love me and because You
have the power to heal,
restore, and revive.

Day 39

Lord, I am thankful to be a citizen of the United States of America. Although my residency is here, my true citizenship is in heaven. Thank You for my "passport," my salvation that allows me entrance into Your kingdom of heaven.

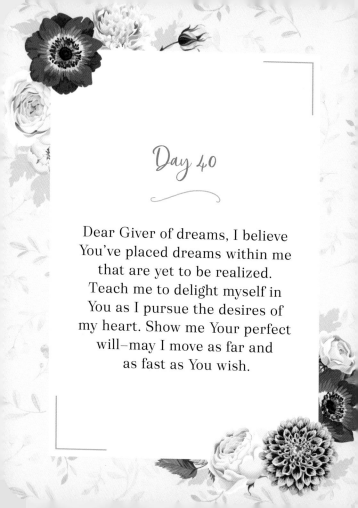

Day 40

Dear Giver of dreams, I believe
You've placed dreams within me
that are yet to be realized.
Teach me to delight myself in
You as I pursue the desires of
my heart. Show me Your perfect
will—may I move as far and
as fast as You wish.

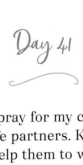

Day 41

Lord, I pray for my children's
future life partners. Keep them
pure and help them to wait for love.
Bring into their lives spouses who
are godly, loving, and supportive.
Give them mates who are well
suited for each other, who will
seek to serve one another
and live in harmony.

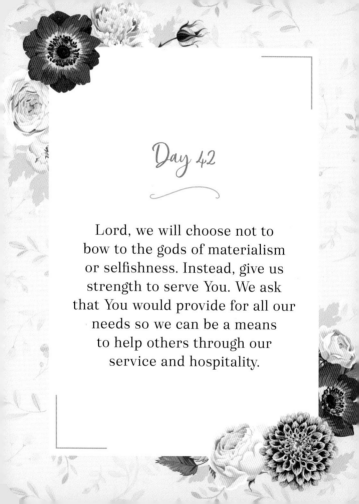

Day 42

Lord, we will choose not to
bow to the gods of materialism
or selfishness. Instead, give us
strength to serve You. We ask
that You would provide for all our
needs so we can be a means
to help others through our
service and hospitality.

Day 43

Lord, the beauty of the earth
reveals Your glory. Thank You for
the smile of a child, the touch of
my beloved's hand, the warmth
of our home. I am grateful for
the love of friends and meaningful
work. Thank You for Your
many blessings.

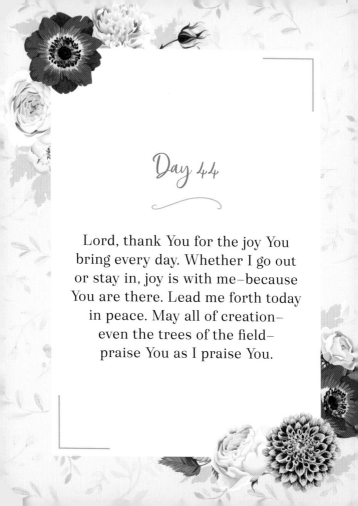

Day 44

Lord, thank You for the joy You
bring every day. Whether I go out
or stay in, joy is with me—because
You are there. Lead me forth today
in peace. May all of creation—
even the trees of the field—
praise You as I praise You.

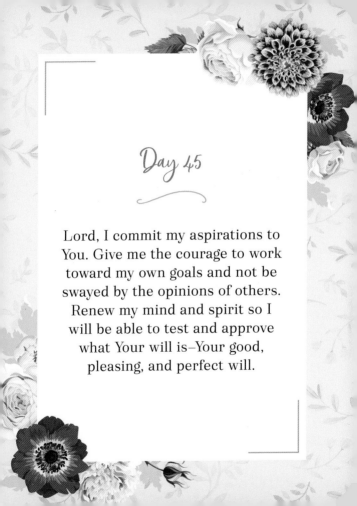

Day 45

Lord, I commit my aspirations to
You. Give me the courage to work
toward my own goals and not be
swayed by the opinions of others.
Renew my mind and spirit so I
will be able to test and approve
what Your will is–Your good,
pleasing, and perfect will.

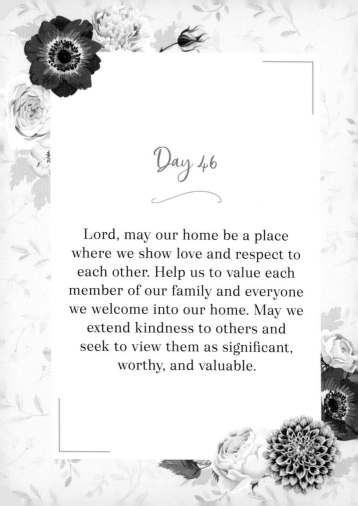

Day 46

Lord, may our home be a place where we show love and respect to each other. Help us to value each member of our family and everyone we welcome into our home. May we extend kindness to others and seek to view them as significant, worthy, and valuable.

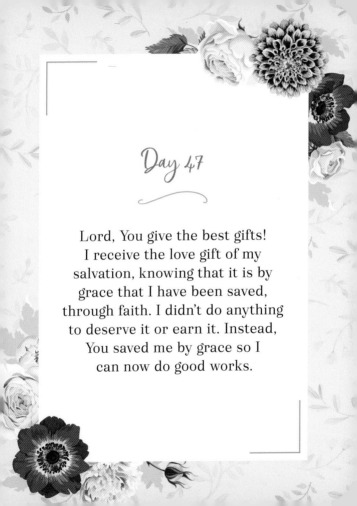

Day 47

Lord, You give the best gifts!
I receive the love gift of my
salvation, knowing that it is by
grace that I have been saved,
through faith. I didn't do anything
to deserve it or earn it. Instead,
You saved me by grace so I
can now do good works.

Day 48

Lord, I need Your times of
refreshing in my life. Bread of
heaven, as You nourish my body
with food, feed my soul with Your
words of comfort and life. May I
be filled with Your healing
love, joy, and goodness.

Day 49

Lord, thank You for my home.
Show me opportunities to open this
home to others. However my home
compares with others', I thank
You for what I have. I am grateful
that Your Spirit is present here.
Give me a generous, open heart,
and use my home for
Your purposes.

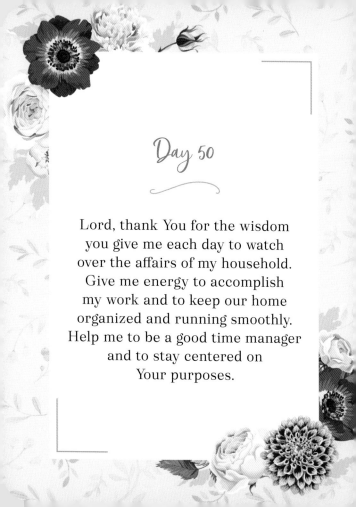

Day 50

Lord, thank You for the wisdom
you give me each day to watch
over the affairs of my household.
Give me energy to accomplish
my work and to keep our home
organized and running smoothly.
Help me to be a good time manager
and to stay centered on
Your purposes.

Day 51

Lord, sometimes I feel like my emotions need a makeover. Renovate me—transform me so I can be balanced and healthy emotionally. I ask for Your power to change. I don't want to be the way I used to be. I want to be wise and enjoy sound thinking.

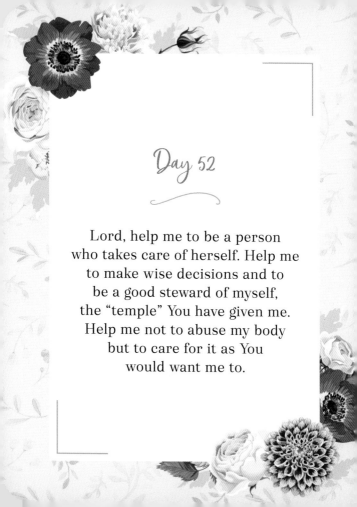

Day 52

Lord, help me to be a person
who takes care of herself. Help me
to make wise decisions and to
be a good steward of myself,
the "temple" You have given me.
Help me not to abuse my body
but to care for it as You
would want me to.

Day 53

Lord, in our family, give us the grace to encourage one another. Help us to build each other up, not tear each other down. Help me to show approval to my children by catching them doing right, not just correcting them when they do something wrong.

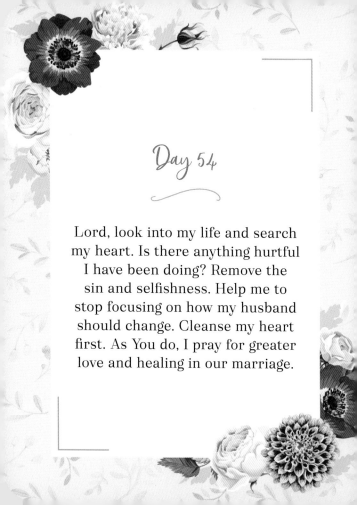

Day 54

Lord, look into my life and search my heart. Is there anything hurtful I have been doing? Remove the sin and selfishness. Help me to stop focusing on how my husband should change. Cleanse my heart first. As You do, I pray for greater love and healing in our marriage.

Day 55

Lord, help me to find relief from stress in my life. I need to value rest and make time to relax. I cast my cares on You, my burden bearer. Help me find joy again in the things I like to do. Calm me and renew me, Lord.

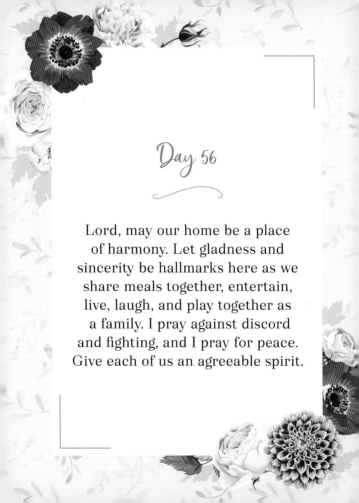

Day 56

Lord, may our home be a place of harmony. Let gladness and sincerity be hallmarks here as we share meals together, entertain, live, laugh, and play together as a family. I pray against discord and fighting, and I pray for peace. Give each of us an agreeable spirit.

Day 57

Lord, I ask that my husband and I
would value each other. As he loves
me, help me to respect him. As I
value him, help him to cherish me.
Teach us to give and to receive in
the ways that are meaningful
to each of us.

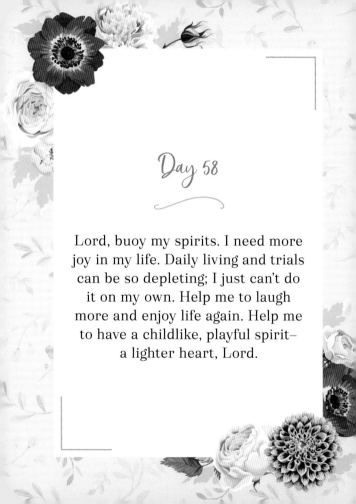

Day 58

Lord, buoy my spirits. I need more
joy in my life. Daily living and trials
can be so depleting; I just can't do
it on my own. Help me to laugh
more and enjoy life again. Help me
to have a childlike, playful spirit–
a lighter heart, Lord.

Day 59

Lord, thank You for the peace that restores me and brings wholeness. When my heart is restless, my health suffers. But when I am at peace, You restore my entire body. I can breathe easier, and I can smile again because I know everything's going to be all right.

Day 60

Lord, I have done many foolish things–and I am sorry. I have made unwise choices, and I have been deceived and taken captive by the passions and pleasures of the world. Forgive me. Thank You for saving me by Your mercy and a love that's hard to fathom.

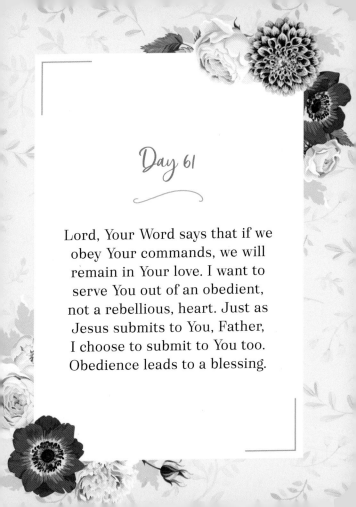

Day 61

Lord, Your Word says that if we obey Your commands, we will remain in Your love. I want to serve You out of an obedient, not a rebellious, heart. Just as Jesus submits to You, Father, I choose to submit to You too. Obedience leads to a blessing.

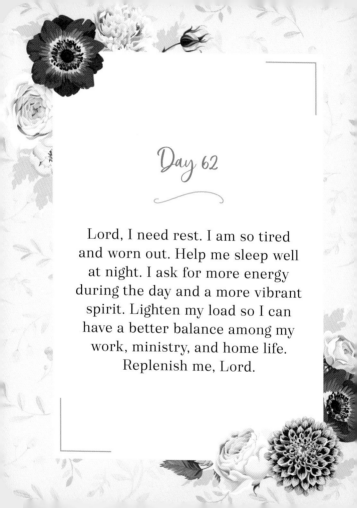

Day 62

Lord, I need rest. I am so tired and worn out. Help me sleep well at night. I ask for more energy during the day and a more vibrant spirit. Lighten my load so I can have a better balance among my work, ministry, and home life. Replenish me, Lord.

Day 63

Lord, I pray that we would speak encouraging and kind words in our home. Help us to build each other up—never to tear each other down. Help us not to be so self-absorbed that we forget to ask how others around us are doing.

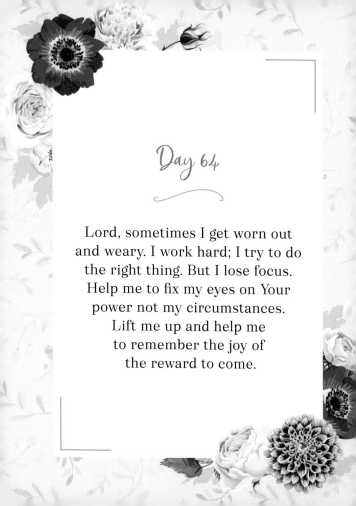

Day 64

Lord, sometimes I get worn out
and weary. I work hard; I try to do
the right thing. But I lose focus.
Help me to fix my eyes on Your
power not my circumstances.
Lift me up and help me
to remember the joy of
the reward to come.

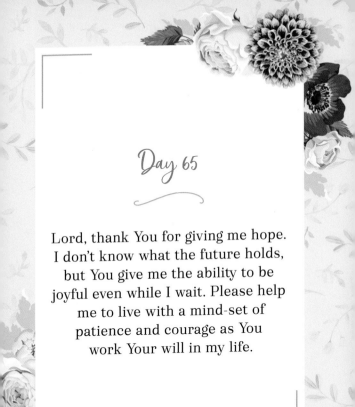

Day 65

Lord, thank You for giving me hope.
I don't know what the future holds,
but You give me the ability to be
joyful even while I wait. Please help
me to live with a mind-set of
patience and courage as You
work Your will in my life.

Day 66

Your Word is my daily
nourishment, Lord. Thank You
for the Bread of Life You provide
every single day. Those words
feed and nurture my soul.
Without Your words I will fade
and die spiritually; with them I
am vibrant, energized, and alive!
Be my portion as I seek You.

Day 67

Lord, You are called Wonderful
Counselor because You freely give
wisdom and guidance. You are the
Mighty God, the One who made the
entire world and keeps it all going.
My Everlasting Father, it's Your
love and compassion that
sustain me. My Prince of Peace,
I worship and honor You.

Day 68

Lord, teach us how to serve one
another. Help us, as we help others,
to be loving and encouraging.
Let us be more aware of the needs
of others–and find delight
in making their load easier.
Help us to serve with a heart
of love and gratitude.

Day 69

Lord, I want our family to pray together more often. We need to put You first because You are the source of life–and You are worthy of our firstfruits of time and attention. Help us make spending time with You a priority.

Day 70

Lord, teach me to read Your Word, meditate on it, and apply it to my life. Give me a hunger for spending time with You—and wisdom when I teach Your Word to others. I want to be a person who correctly handles the Word of Truth.

Day 71

Lord, I need more time—and
motivation—to get in shape. I want
to have a fitness routine, but my
schedule is crazy. Show me how to
make movement a priority so I will
feel better, look better, and have
more energy. I want to honor
You with my body.

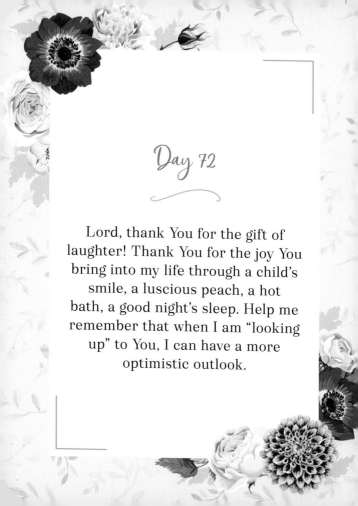

Day 72

Lord, thank You for the gift of laughter! Thank You for the joy You bring into my life through a child's smile, a luscious peach, a hot bath, a good night's sleep. Help me remember that when I am "looking up" to You, I can have a more optimistic outlook.

Day 73

Lord, make me a tool of Your peace. Instead of the hammer of judgment, let me bring the balm of love. Instead of bitterness and resentment, help me to quickly forgive. When doubt misaligns my emotions, level me with faith. When I cannot find an answer, let me know Your great hope.

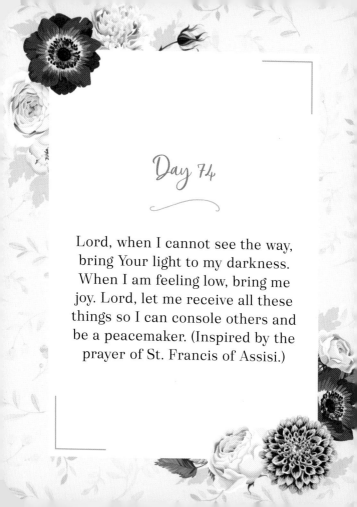

Day 74

Lord, when I cannot see the way,
bring Your light to my darkness.
When I am feeling low, bring me
joy. Lord, let me receive all these
things so I can console others and
be a peacemaker. (Inspired by the
prayer of St. Francis of Assisi.)

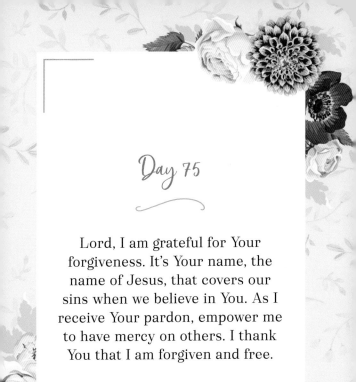

Day 75

Lord, I am grateful for Your forgiveness. It's Your name, the name of Jesus, that covers our sins when we believe in You. As I receive Your pardon, empower me to have mercy on others. I thank You that I am forgiven and free.

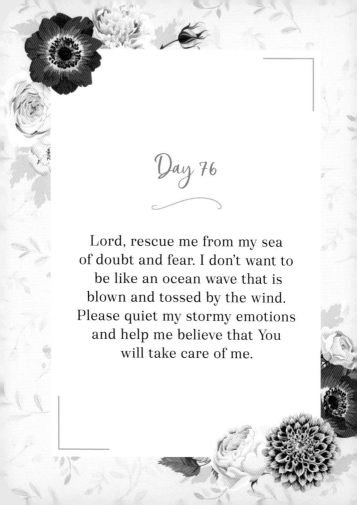

Day 76

Lord, rescue me from my sea
of doubt and fear. I don't want to
be like an ocean wave that is
blown and tossed by the wind.
Please quiet my stormy emotions
and help me believe that You
will take care of me.

Day 77

Lord, I need Your strength.
Stronger than steel, Your character
is so solid I don't have to be afraid.
You are with me–and that means
everything. I can have joy because
of Your joy in me. With Your
righteous right hand You help
me, deliver me, and uphold me.

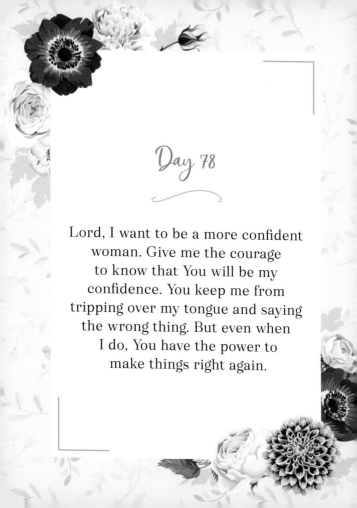

Day 78

Lord, I want to be a more confident
woman. Give me the courage
to know that You will be my
confidence. You keep me from
tripping over my tongue and saying
the wrong thing. But even when
I do, You have the power to
make things right again.

Day 79

Lord, I have looked for approval from others for too long. I long for the acceptance of other people– and am more often than not disappointed. Forgive me. I want to trust in You. Deliver me from this hunger for human approval. Bring me into the freedom of Your grace.

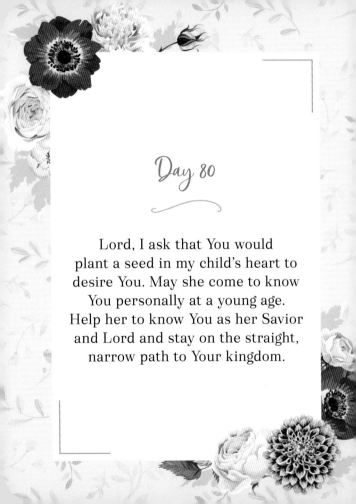

Day 80

Lord, I ask that You would
plant a seed in my child's heart to
desire You. May she come to know
You personally at a young age.
Help her to know You as her Savior
and Lord and stay on the straight,
narrow path to Your kingdom.

Day 81

Lord, You give me many good gifts—
but I know that fear is not one of
them. You have given me a spirit
of power, love, and self-discipline—
power to do Your will, to love
others, and to discipline myself
to think about things that
lead me into faith.

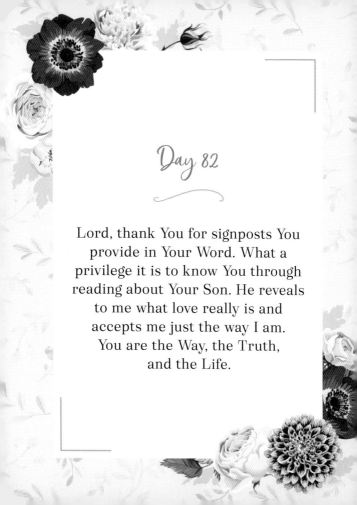

Day 82

Lord, thank You for signposts You
provide in Your Word. What a
privilege it is to know You through
reading about Your Son. He reveals
to me what love really is and
accepts me just the way I am.
You are the Way, the Truth,
and the Life.

Day 83

Lord, I am so tired of imitations.
It's hard to tell what is false and
what is true anymore. When it
comes to joy, I want the real thing.
I need more of You, Lord. I pray for
righteousness, peace, and joy in
the Holy Spirit. Fill me, please.

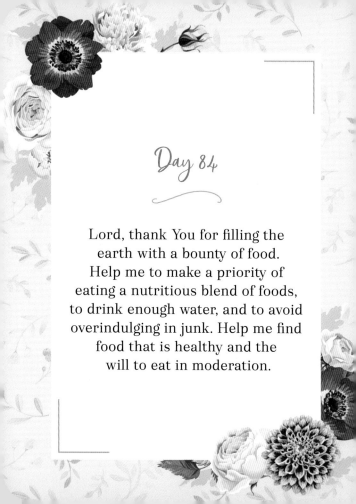

Day 84

Lord, thank You for filling the
earth with a bounty of food.
Help me to make a priority of
eating a nutritious blend of foods,
to drink enough water, and to avoid
overindulging in junk. Help me find
food that is healthy and the
will to eat in moderation.

Day 85

Lord, thank You for the household
You have entrusted to my care.
Help me to be a wise steward
of all that You have provided.
May we use our money wisely,
share freely of Your blessings,
and spend our time toward
positive ends that bring
glory to Your name.

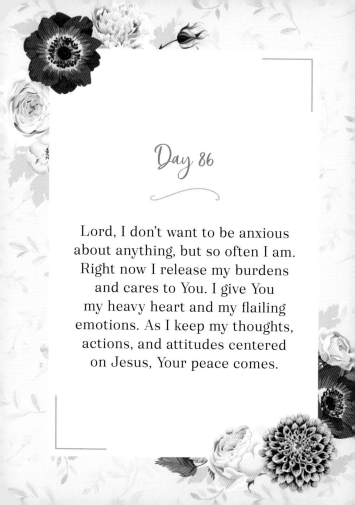

Day 86

Lord, I don't want to be anxious about anything, but so often I am. Right now I release my burdens and cares to You. I give You my heavy heart and my flailing emotions. As I keep my thoughts, actions, and attitudes centered on Jesus, Your peace comes.

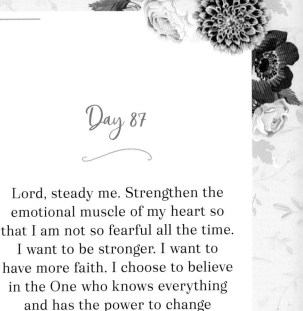

Day 87

Lord, steady me. Strengthen the
emotional muscle of my heart so
that I am not so fearful all the time.
I want to be stronger. I want to
have more faith. I choose to believe
in the One who knows everything
and has the power to change
hearts and lives.

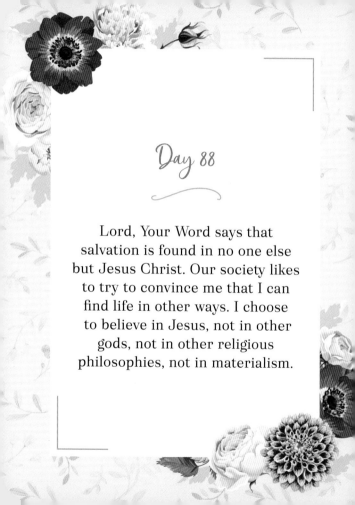

Day 88

Lord, Your Word says that
salvation is found in no one else
but Jesus Christ. Our society likes
to try to convince me that I can
find life in other ways. I choose
to believe in Jesus, not in other
gods, not in other religious
philosophies, not in materialism.

Day 89

Lord, keep me safe in Your dwelling place. Hide me from my enemies in Your secure shelter. Comfort me with Your warm blanket of peace and love. I am safe with You, and in Your presence I can move from fearful to fearless, from timid to trusting.

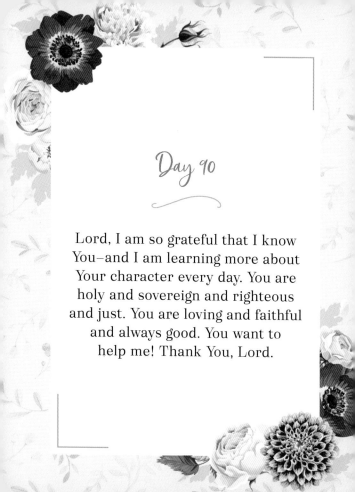

Day 90

Lord, I am so grateful that I know You—and I am learning more about Your character every day. You are holy and sovereign and righteous and just. You are loving and faithful and always good. You want to help me! Thank You, Lord.

Day 91

Lord, plant Your wisdom in me
like seeds in the soil. Help me
cultivate each one and follow Your
ways. They are pure, peace-loving,
considerate, submissive, full of
mercy and good fruit, impartial,
and sincere. May I be a person
who sows in peace and raises
a harvest of righteousness.

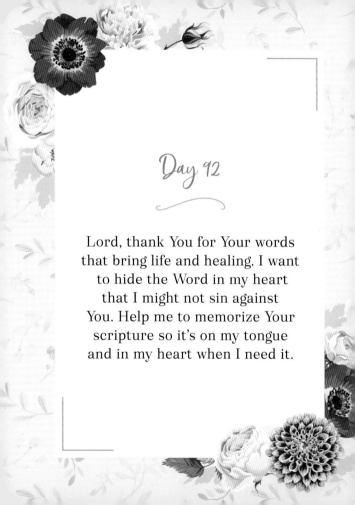

Day 92

Lord, thank You for Your words
that bring life and healing. I want
to hide the Word in my heart
that I might not sin against
You. Help me to memorize Your
scripture so it's on my tongue
and in my heart when I need it.

Day 93

Lord, thank You for the joy and
privilege of praying for others.
What a blessing to be able to
intercede, to stand in the gap
and move heaven and earth
for those I love. In all my
prayers for those I know,
may I have a heart of joy.

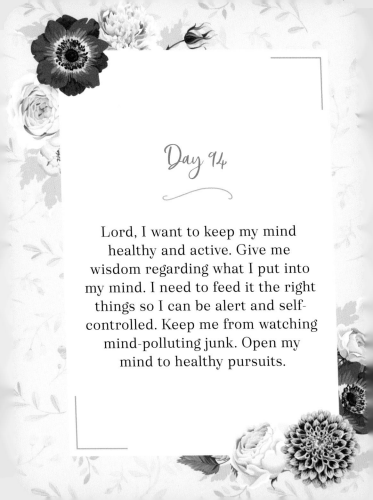

Day 94

Lord, I want to keep my mind healthy and active. Give me wisdom regarding what I put into my mind. I need to feed it the right things so I can be alert and self-controlled. Keep me from watching mind-polluting junk. Open my mind to healthy pursuits.

Day 95

Lord, help me to be a wife of noble character. I want to be valuable to my husband. May he have full confidence in me as I seek to bring him good all the days of my life. Clothe me with strength and dignity. Help me to be faithful.

Day 96

Lord, everyone is looking for peace.
Your Word tells us it's not what we
eat or drink that provides lasting
satisfaction. May I find peace and
joy in Your Holy Spirit. Knowing
You, loving You, and experiencing
You is true peace. Thank You, Lord.

Day 97

Lord, help me to find my
contentment in You. I don't
want to be defined by "stuff."
May my greatest happiness in
life be knowing who You are
and who I am in Christ. May I
treasure the simple things in
life, those things that
bring me peace.

Day 98

Lord, often I am afraid. In the dark, challenging times of my life, I can't always see the way. But You are light! Thank You that the darkness is as light to You, so I don't have to be afraid. No matter what happens, I will be confident in You.

Day 99

Lord, I don't just want to hear or read the Bible; I want to do what it says. I want to live what I believe! Help me not to be deceived or forget what my eyes have just read. I look to Your Word and ask for Your blessings.

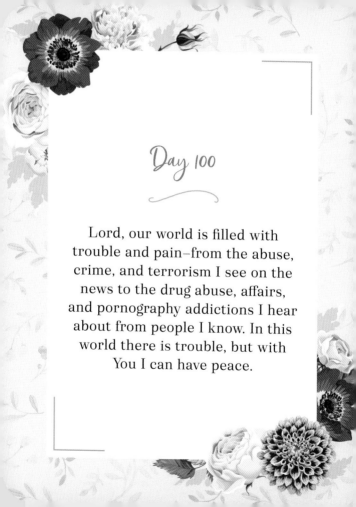

Day 100

Lord, our world is filled with trouble and pain—from the abuse, crime, and terrorism I see on the news to the drug abuse, affairs, and pornography addictions I hear about from people I know. In this world there is trouble, but with You I can have peace.

Day 101

Lord, there is none like You.
When I am sad, You are my
comfort. Your calm presence
restores my soul. Your words are
cool, refreshing water to my spirit.
Despite my confusion, You guide
me in paths of righteousness,
and it's all for Your glory.

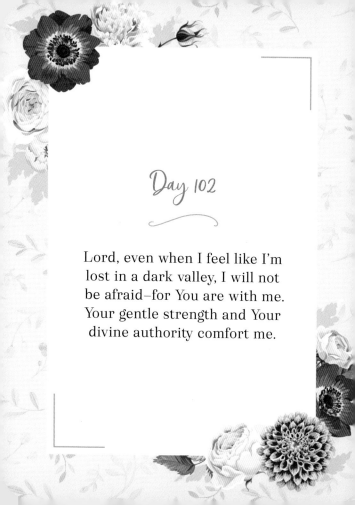

Day 102

Lord, even when I feel like I'm
lost in a dark valley, I will not
be afraid—for You are with me.
Your gentle strength and Your
divine authority comfort me.

Day 103

Lord, I need Your help in dealing with my anger. Help me to process my emotions and not let them fester. Help me to control my temper and talk about what bothers me in calmer ways, to give You my anger so I can live in peace with my husband.

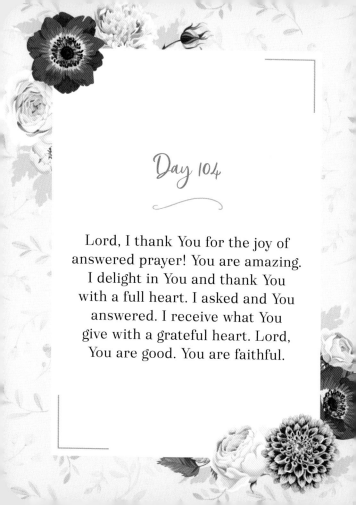

Day 104

Lord, I thank You for the joy of
answered prayer! You are amazing.
I delight in You and thank You
with a full heart. I asked and You
answered. I receive what You
give with a grateful heart. Lord,
You are good. You are faithful.

Day 105

Lord, thank You for my work.
My occupation gives me the ability
to shape lives and influence people
every day. Thank You for the ability
to be a "missionary" wherever my
feet tread. Season my words so
that others may taste and see
that my Lord is good.

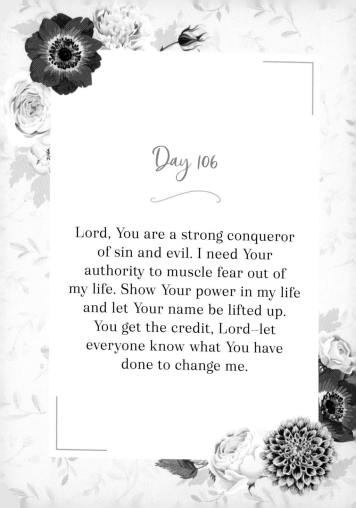

Day 106

Lord, You are a strong conqueror of sin and evil. I need Your authority to muscle fear out of my life. Show Your power in my life and let Your name be lifted up. You get the credit, Lord—let everyone know what You have done to change me.

Day 107

Lord, thank You for all the
emotions we have. Help me to enjoy
stable and good emotional health.
I pray for wholeness in my feelings.
I pray that I would have more
confidence and that I would
find my competence in You.

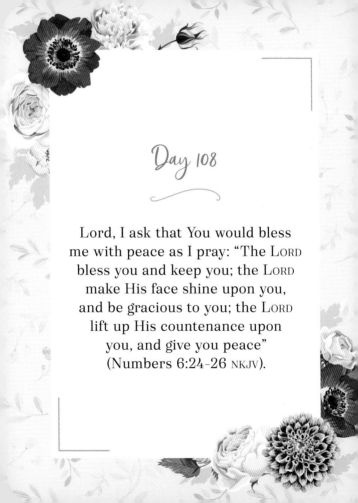

Day 108

Lord, I ask that You would bless
me with peace as I pray: "The LORD
bless you and keep you; the LORD
make His face shine upon you,
and be gracious to you; the LORD
lift up His countenance upon
you, and give you peace"
(Numbers 6:24-26 NKJV).

Day 109

Lord, will You please inspire my heart and strengthen me? I need Your truth to lift my spirit and help me soar. Let me be like an eagle that glides on the wind. Give me the courage and energy I need to keep going even when I'm weary.

Day 110

Lord, I need wisdom and guidance
in my work life. Please show me
if this is the vocation I should be
in right now or if I should find
another job. I want to use my
skills and abilities, as well as my
interests, for Your glory.

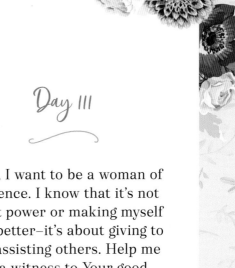

Day 111

Lord, I want to be a woman of influence. I know that it's not about power or making myself look better–it's about giving to and assisting others. Help me be a witness to Your good things in my life.

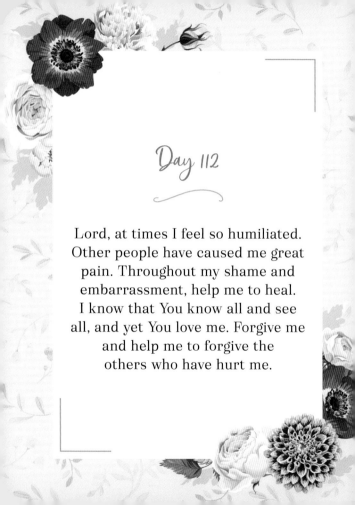

Day 112

Lord, at times I feel so humiliated.
Other people have caused me great
pain. Throughout my shame and
embarrassment, help me to heal.
I know that You know all and see
all, and yet You love me. Forgive me
and help me to forgive the
others who have hurt me.

Day 113

Lord, thank You for Your
protection of my children.
With the full armor of God,
may they be strong in Your mighty
power. Help them to stand firm
with the belt of truth and to
put on the breastplate of
righteousness, knowing they
are in right standing with You.

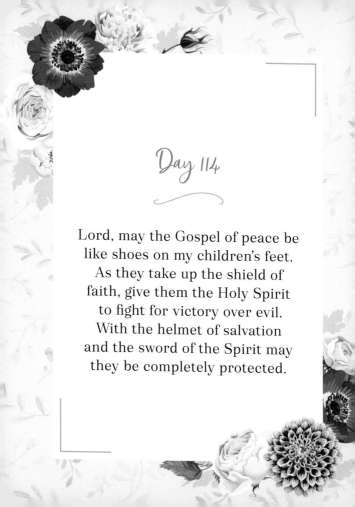

Day 114

Lord, may the Gospel of peace be
like shoes on my children's feet.
As they take up the shield of
faith, give them the Holy Spirit
to fight for victory over evil.
With the helmet of salvation
and the sword of the Spirit may
they be completely protected.

Day 115

Lord, draw me closer to You.
In Your presence is fullness of
joy–and I want to be filled. Knowing
I am loved by You makes me glad;
I cannot imagine life without You.
With You there is light; without
You, darkness. With You there is
pleasure; without You, pain.

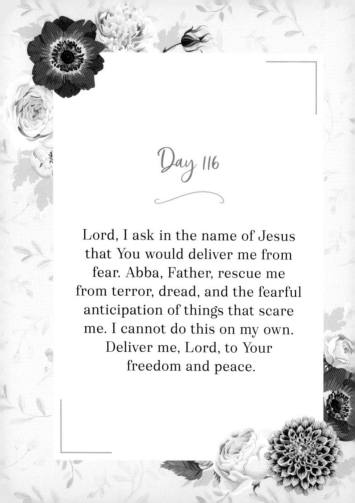

Day 116

Lord, I ask in the name of Jesus that You would deliver me from fear. Abba, Father, rescue me from terror, dread, and the fearful anticipation of things that scare me. I cannot do this on my own. Deliver me, Lord, to Your freedom and peace.

Day 117

Lord, I feel so gloomy today.
Do You see my tears? In my
sadness, help me to remember
that even when I'm down, I can
choose to put my hope in You.
Instead of telling myself lies that
push me deeper into despair,
I can look to Your truth.

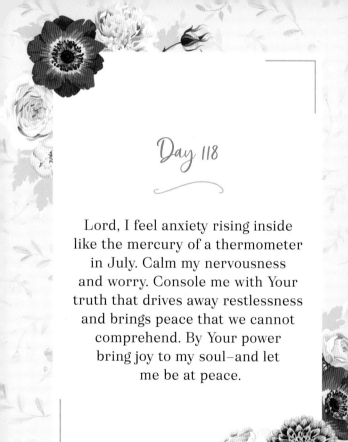

Day 118

Lord, I feel anxiety rising inside
like the mercury of a thermometer
in July. Calm my nervousness
and worry. Console me with Your
truth that drives away restlessness
and brings peace that we cannot
comprehend. By Your power
bring joy to my soul—and let
me be at peace.

Day 119

Lord, You give me work to do every day. Whether it's at home or in the marketplace, help me to honor You in my efforts. I don't want to be satisfied with mediocrity. I ask that You would empower me to do superior work and bring glory to Your name.

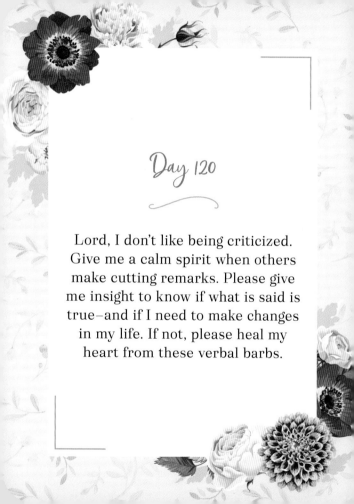

Day 120

Lord, I don't like being criticized.
Give me a calm spirit when others
make cutting remarks. Please give
me insight to know if what is said is
true–and if I need to make changes
in my life. If not, please heal my
heart from these verbal barbs.

Day 121

Lord, teach me to be a leader
by being a servant. Strange as
it may seem, You say that
"whoever desires to become
great among you shall be
your servant" (Mark 10:43 NKJV).
Help me to be more like Christ,
as He did not come to be
served but to serve.

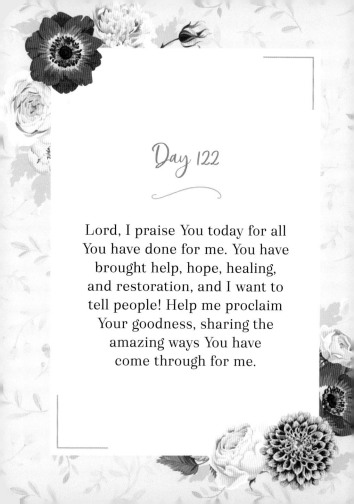

Day 122

Lord, I praise You today for all You have done for me. You have brought help, hope, healing, and restoration, and I want to tell people! Help me proclaim Your goodness, sharing the amazing ways You have come through for me.

Day 123

Lord, I thank You that You value the calling of motherhood. As I work to serve my family and build our house into a home, I pray for wisdom, endurance, energy, and joy. Help me to know that raising children is a significant and high honor.

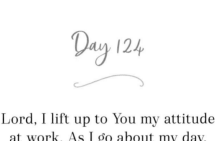

Day 124

Lord, I lift up to You my attitude
at work. As I go about my day,
may I have a positive outlook and
a helpful spirit. Help me to be
encouraging to others. Amid the
activity, may my heart be at
peace as the Holy Spirit
strengthens and empowers me.

Day 125

Lord, help me to be a good role model as I teach my kids to pray. As a spiritual coach, empower me to pray for them and with them. May I provide clear instruction and a consistent example so my children can form good prayer habits.

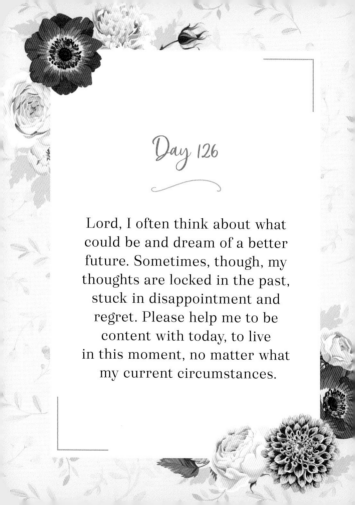

Day 126

Lord, I often think about what could be and dream of a better future. Sometimes, though, my thoughts are locked in the past, stuck in disappointment and regret. Please help me to be content with today, to live in this moment, no matter what my current circumstances.

Day 127

Lord, I am thankful for the
financial resources with which
You have blessed me. I want to be
a good steward, a wise manager,
of the resources You have
entrusted to me. Help me to
save and spend with discernment
and to give to others in need.

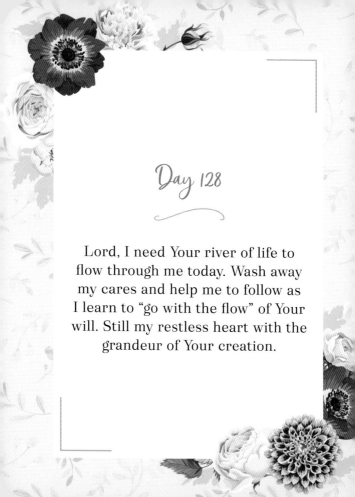

Day 128

Lord, I need Your river of life to flow through me today. Wash away my cares and help me to follow as I learn to "go with the flow" of Your will. Still my restless heart with the grandeur of Your creation.

Day 129

Lord, we need Your help to get rid of bitterness and anger in our marriage. Help us to build each other up instead of putting each other down. Help us to forgive one another and to be kind and compassionate, because we know Christ forgave each of us.

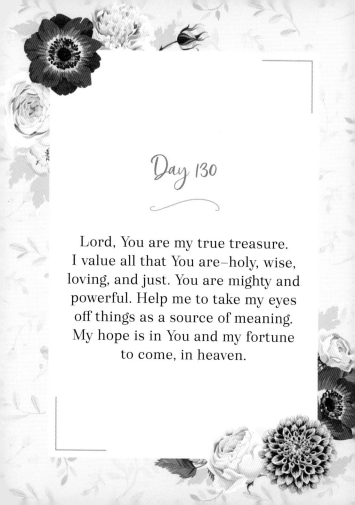

Day 130

Lord, You are my true treasure.
I value all that You are—holy, wise,
loving, and just. You are mighty and
powerful. Help me to take my eyes
off things as a source of meaning.
My hope is in You and my fortune
to come, in heaven.

Day 131

Lord, please bless the work of my hands. As I sit at a computer or fold laundry or teach a classroom of children, may my work be meaningful and bear good fruit. I pray for a spirit of joy during the day as I go about my business.

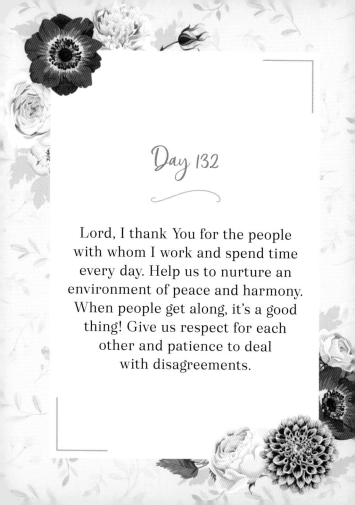

Day 132

Lord, I thank You for the people with whom I work and spend time every day. Help us to nurture an environment of peace and harmony. When people get along, it's a good thing! Give us respect for each other and patience to deal with disagreements.

Day 133

Lord, we ask You for wisdom
and harmony in our financial life.
We choose to serve You. Forgive us
when we have been selfish, when
we've gone to extremes of spending
or hoarding. Heal us when we need
restoration in our finances.

Day 134

Lord, thank You for my church and my brothers and sisters in Christ. May we grow together as a "family" of believers as we learn to love and serve each other. Although we are different, help us to respect each other and seek to build up one another.

Day 135

Lord, I am so grateful that You are helping me become a person who walks in peace. Mentor me in Your ways so I can live in harmony and be a positive example for others. I don't want to put anyone down; I want to build them up.

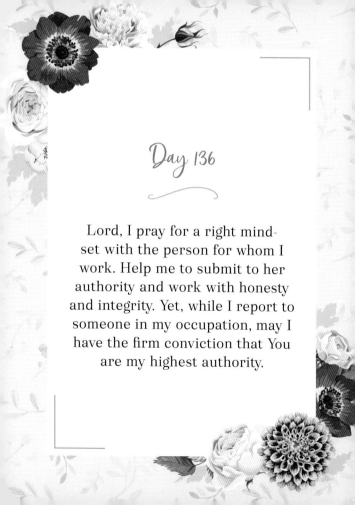

Day 136

Lord, I pray for a right mind-set with the person for whom I work. Help me to submit to her authority and work with honesty and integrity. Yet, while I report to someone in my occupation, may I have the firm conviction that You are my highest authority.

Day 137

Lord, please give me discernment to spend money sensibly. I know from Your Word that money itself is not evil; it's the love of money–greed–that makes us wander from the faith. Help me to spend the money You provide not in self-indulgence but in good judgment.

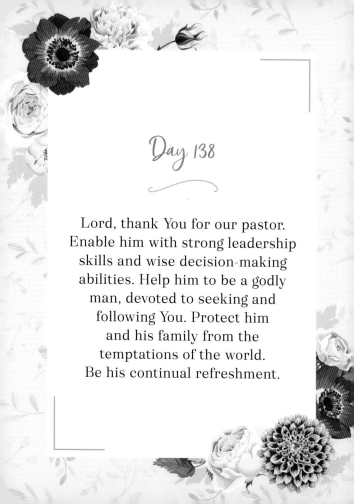

Day 138

Lord, thank You for our pastor.
Enable him with strong leadership
skills and wise decision-making
abilities. Help him to be a godly
man, devoted to seeking and
following You. Protect him
and his family from the
temptations of the world.
Be his continual refreshment.

Day 139

Lord, will you please change
the music of my life from a sad,
minor key to a joy-filled, major key?
Give me a new song to sing,
a happier tune! As You lift me
from the mire of my depression
to solid emotional ground,
I will praise You.

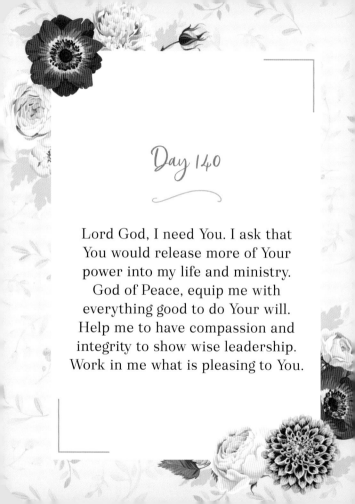

Day 140

Lord God, I need You. I ask that You would release more of Your power into my life and ministry. God of Peace, equip me with everything good to do Your will. Help me to have compassion and integrity to show wise leadership. Work in me what is pleasing to You.

Day 141

Lord, I'm tired. I have been doing too much, and I need rest. Help me to manage my priorities–my home life, work, ministry, and rest–in better ways so I have more balance and less stress. I don't want to get burned out but be effective for You.

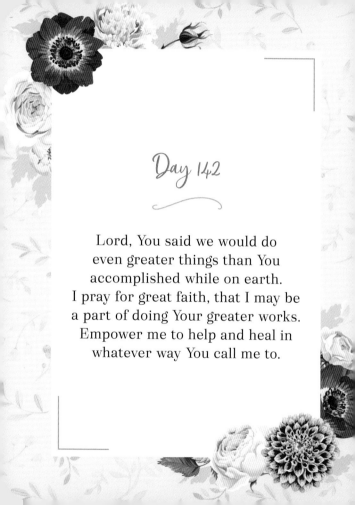

Day 142

Lord, You said we would do
even greater things than You
accomplished while on earth.
I pray for great faith, that I may be
a part of doing Your greater works.
Empower me to help and heal in
whatever way You call me to.

Day 143

Lord, I want to live a clean, healthy life. As I abide in Your Word, help me to be pure in my thought life and in my body. Help me provide a healthy environment in my home with less dirt and dust and fewer germs.

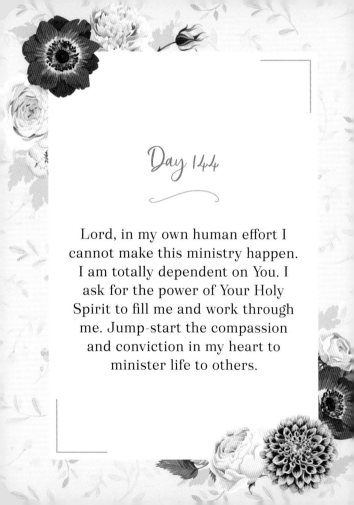

Day 144

Lord, in my own human effort I cannot make this ministry happen. I am totally dependent on You. I ask for the power of Your Holy Spirit to fill me and work through me. Jump-start the compassion and conviction in my heart to minister life to others.

Day 145

Lord, I thank You for the blessings and joys my friends bring to my life. Thank You for my "heart" friends, who listen, care, and encourage me. I acknowledge that You are the Giver of all good gifts, and I thank You for Your provision in my friendships.

Day 146

Lord, I appreciate Your wise hand of guidance. You instruct me and teach me in the way I should go; You counsel me and watch over me. No one knows my inner heart and life dreams like You. Help me to listen so I can hear Your direction.

Day 147

Lord, I ask for insight into
the people I serve. Give me
understanding as to their needs
so I can better interact with them.
Help me to take an interest in their
culture, whether ethnic or age
related. Give me wisdom on how
to reach them, teach them,
and bless them.

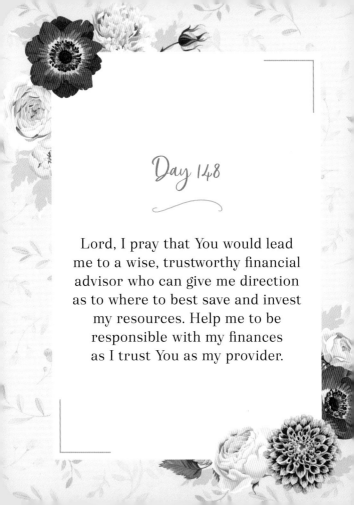

Day 148

Lord, I pray that You would lead
me to a wise, trustworthy financial
advisor who can give me direction
as to where to best save and invest
my resources. Help me to be
responsible with my finances
as I trust You as my provider.

Day 149

Lord, You are my strength—please
protect me. You are my safety—
preserve me. Keep me safe in Your
tender care as I minister to the
needs of others. And please protect
those around me, the ones to
whom I minister. Bless me and
keep me from my enemies.

Day 150

Lord, I ask that my extended family members will know and experience Your wisdom each day. May they find that wisdom is more precious than rubies and that godly understanding is better than gold. Nothing they desire on earth can compare with knowing You and following Your ways.

Day 151

Lord, sometimes it's such a temptation to talk about other people. Show me the line between relating needed information and gossiping–passing along rumors that may hurt a friend or family member. Help me to be a woman who can keep a secret and not betray a confidence.

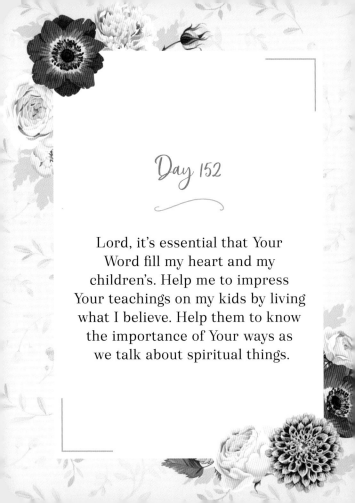

Day 152

Lord, it's essential that Your Word fill my heart and my children's. Help me to impress Your teachings on my kids by living what I believe. Help them to know the importance of Your ways as we talk about spiritual things.

Day 153

Lord, I'm feeling envious–
and I need Your help. Wherever
I look I see people who have
something more or better than
I do, and that makes me struggle
inside. Take away this jealousy
and help me to be content,
knowing that You will
provide for all my needs.

Day 154

Lord, help our family to be more encouraging. Where we've been silent, please bring kind words of praise. Where we've been angry, bring words of peace. Help me to be a person who lifts up others by saying kind, appreciative, worthwhile things.

Day 155

Lord, I ask in Jesus' name that my unsaved friend would come to know You as her personal Savior. I pray for her salvation and for her growth in faith. As You reveal Yourself to her, may she come to truly experience You.

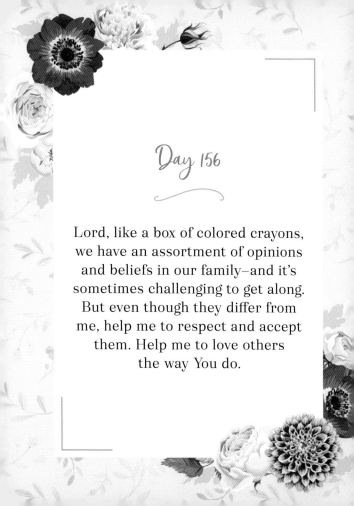

Day 156

Lord, like a box of colored crayons,
we have an assortment of opinions
and beliefs in our family—and it's
sometimes challenging to get along.
But even though they differ from
me, help me to respect and accept
them. Help me to love others
the way You do.

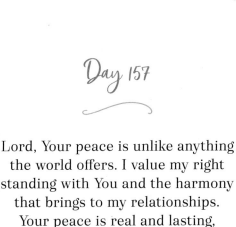

Day 157

Lord, Your peace is unlike anything
the world offers. I value my right
standing with You and the harmony
that brings to my relationships.
Your peace is real and lasting,
never to be taken away. I thank
You that Your peace brings life.

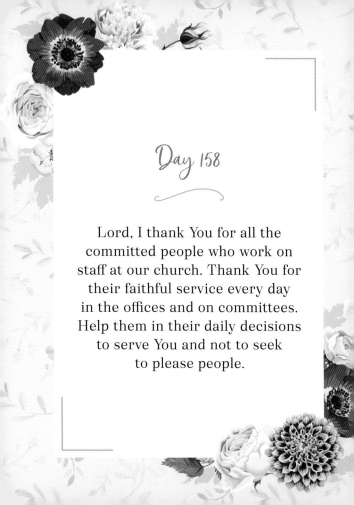

Day 158

Lord, I thank You for all the
committed people who work on
staff at our church. Thank You for
their faithful service every day
in the offices and on committees.
Help them in their daily decisions
to serve You and not to seek
to please people.

Day 159

Lord, I thank You for my family members and those who are like family to me. I am grateful for their love and understanding. May I be loving in return–not only to those who love me but even to those who are hard to be around.

Day 160

Lord, please give me the self-control and motivation I need to make wise choices to support the health of my mind, my spirit, and my body. I want to be a woman of balance, not extremes. Help me to be a wise steward of this resource You've given me.

Day 161

Lord, You are the Author of love. When the challenges of life come, help my husband and me to love and support each other with empathy, kindness, and love. Protect our love and keep our marriage solid as we put our hope and trust in You.

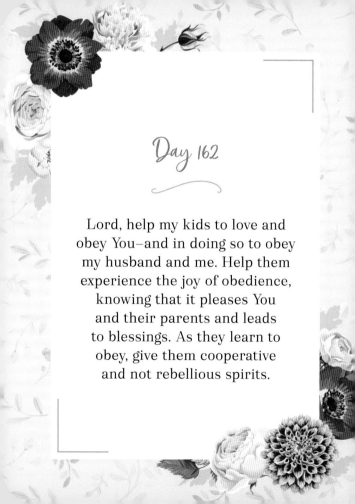

Day 162

Lord, help my kids to love and obey You—and in doing so to obey my husband and me. Help them experience the joy of obedience, knowing that it pleases You and their parents and leads to blessings. As they learn to obey, give them cooperative and not rebellious spirits.

Day 163

Lord, I pray for a spirit of
compassion. Help me to care
about the needs of others and have
genuine love for the ones I serve.
Pour into me Your caring, kind
Spirit so I can be a blessing and
minister out of a full heart.

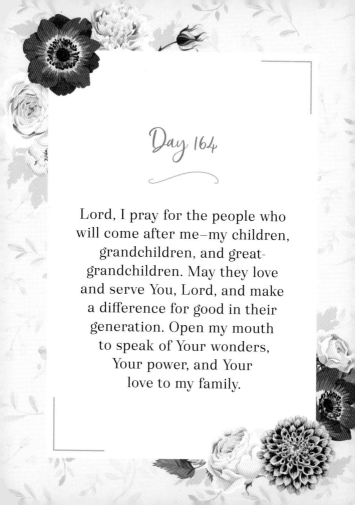

Day 164

Lord, I pray for the people who will come after me—my children, grandchildren, and great-grandchildren. May they love and serve You, Lord, and make a difference for good in their generation. Open my mouth to speak of Your wonders, Your power, and Your love to my family.

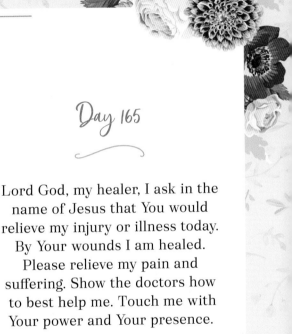

Day 165

Lord God, my healer, I ask in the name of Jesus that You would relieve my injury or illness today. By Your wounds I am healed. Please relieve my pain and suffering. Show the doctors how to best help me. Touch me with Your power and Your presence.

Day 166

Lord, I want to be a person
of peace and live in harmony
with others. I know my family
members and I don't always agree.
But when we disagree, help us to
work through our differences and
connect again with each other.

Day 167

Lord, teach me to pray. And please help our family members to pray for each other. May we be focused, fervent, and faithful in coming boldly before You. Stir within each of us how best to pray for one another. Help us to develop oneness as we intercede.

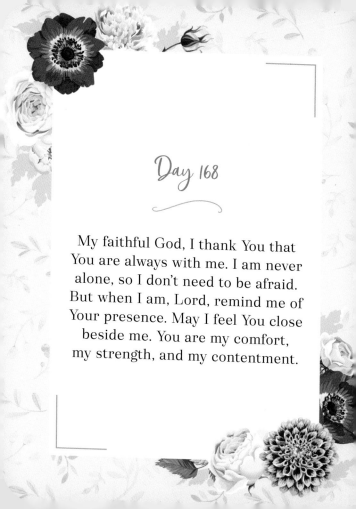

Day 168

My faithful God, I thank You that
You are always with me. I am never
alone, so I don't need to be afraid.
But when I am, Lord, remind me of
Your presence. May I feel You close
beside me. You are my comfort,
my strength, and my contentment.

Day 169

Lord, I pray in the name and power
of Jesus that You would draw my
family member into Your heart.
May she come to know Jesus as
Savior and Lord–soon. Help her
to know Your amazing love,
Your encouraging hope,
and Your healing power.

Day 170

Lord, I humbly ask that we would be united and strong as a couple. May Your cords of peace, honor, respect, and love hold us together during both the good times and the challenges. As we become more connected to You, help us to be closer to each other.

Day 171

Lord, thank You for bringing into
my life people I can call "family"—
beyond those to whom I am related.
Help our relationships to be loving
and encouraging. Give me grace,
Lord, to treat my brothers and
sisters as I myself would
like to be treated.

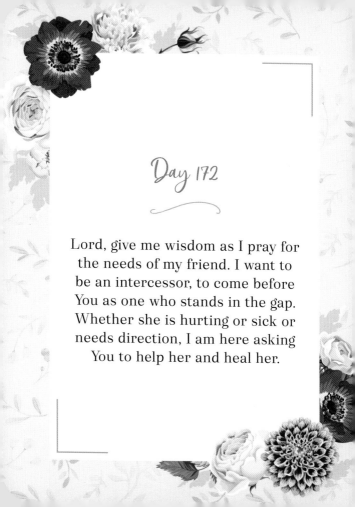

Day 172

Lord, give me wisdom as I pray for the needs of my friend. I want to be an intercessor, to come before You as one who stands in the gap. Whether she is hurting or sick or needs direction, I am here asking You to help her and heal her.

Day 173

Lord, Your resources are
unlimited. I boldly ask that You
would provide for the needs of my
ministry. Bring this ministry to the
minds of people who are willing to
give of their time, money, talents,
or other resources to bless these
ministry efforts to further
Your kingdom.

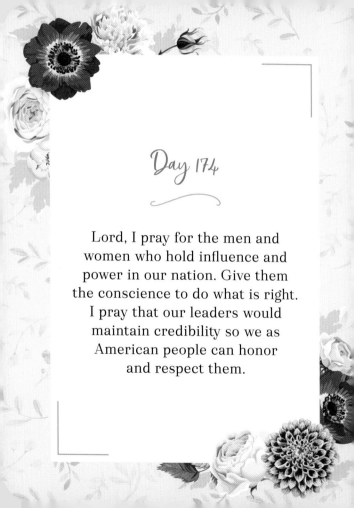

Day 174

Lord, I pray for the men and women who hold influence and power in our nation. Give them the conscience to do what is right. I pray that our leaders would maintain credibility so we as American people can honor and respect them.

Day 175

Lord, teach me Your ways.
Show me how to be a leader who
is first a servant. You showed
us servant leadership when You
washed the feet of Your disciples.
Humble, I come, Lord—let me
be more like You. Deal with my
pride and sin and selfishness.

Day 176

Lord, bless the people who provide
for us as worship leaders, ushers,
greeters, sound and media workers,
and the entire church ministry
team. Bless the kitchen workers,
nursery workers, and others—all
the people in front or behind
the scenes who keep our church
running smoothly and well.

Day 177

Lord, what a blessing it is to be able to come before You–the wisest, most intelligent Being in the universe. I have direct access, straight to the top. Thank You for giving me wisdom and direction, even when I can't see the way.

Day 178

Lord, I don't always know what
to pray for my extended family.
But You know each of them—their
hopes and dreams, needs and
desires. I ask You to intercede
with the power of Your Holy Spirit.
May His deep groans translate
into the words I can't express.

Day 179

Lord, I want things to be different in my life—but there are so many obstacles. I need energy and motivation to get going. I need finances and more time. More than anything, I need to trust You more. Nothing is too difficult for You, Father. You can do anything!

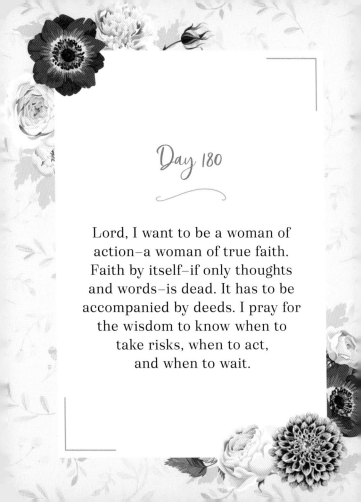

Day 180

Lord, I want to be a woman of
action–a woman of true faith.
Faith by itself–if only thoughts
and words–is dead. It has to be
accompanied by deeds. I pray for
the wisdom to know when to
take risks, when to act,
and when to wait.

Day 181

Lord, reveal to me Your good plans
for my life. As I share my dreams
and visions with You, form them
into reality–or mold them like clay
on a potter's wheel into something
more than I ever could have asked
or imagined. I put my trust in You.

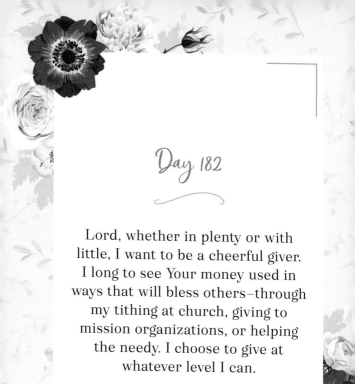

Day 182

Lord, whether in plenty or with little, I want to be a cheerful giver. I long to see Your money used in ways that will bless others—through my tithing at church, giving to mission organizations, or helping the needy. I choose to give at whatever level I can.

Day 183

Lord, the world is our mission field. The harvest is plentiful, and the workers are few–but I ask You, Lord of the harvest, to bring out people with hearts to serve. May they help my ministry and others in our nation and around the world.

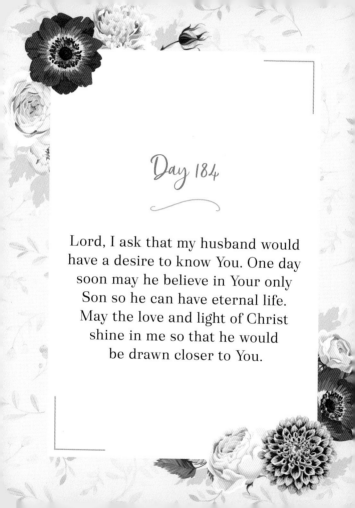

Day 184

Lord, I ask that my husband would
have a desire to know You. One day
soon may he believe in Your only
Son so he can have eternal life.
May the love and light of Christ
shine in me so that he would
be drawn closer to You.

Day 185

I thank You, Lord, for this great
nation. You have blessed America!
Thank You for peace and the
freedom to speak and be heard
and vote for our leaders. Help us
to uphold godly values as we seek
to honor the authority of those
who govern our land.

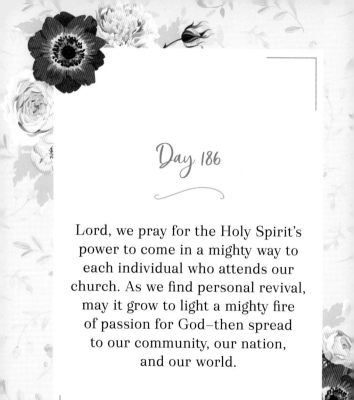

Day 186

Lord, we pray for the Holy Spirit's power to come in a mighty way to each individual who attends our church. As we find personal revival, may it grow to light a mighty fire of passion for God—then spread to our community, our nation, and our world.

Day 187

Lord, help me to be honest as I communicate about my finances—my salary, my savings, my debt, my loans, and my taxes—with the man I share my life with. In all our dealings with money, help us to have integrity.

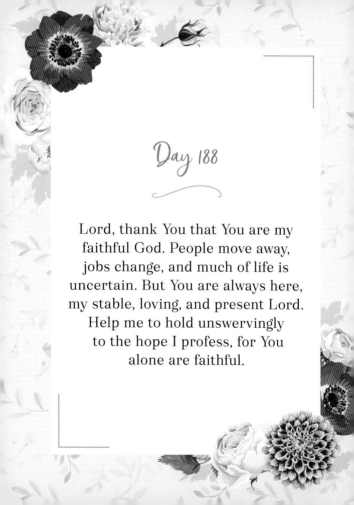

Day 188

Lord, thank You that You are my
faithful God. People move away,
jobs change, and much of life is
uncertain. But You are always here,
my stable, loving, and present Lord.
Help me to hold unswervingly
to the hope I profess, for You
alone are faithful.

Day 189

Lord, I pray for our nation's leaders
and ask that You would give them
the ability to make wise decisions,
to govern with integrity, and to
accomplish their tasks in ways that
build up our nation. May they bring
glory and honor to Your name
as they serve our country.

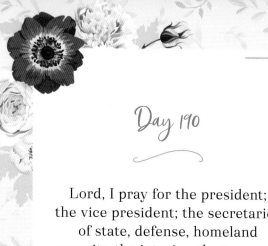

Day 190

Lord, I pray for the president;
the vice president; the secretaries
of state, defense, homeland
security, the interior, the treasury,
agriculture, commerce, labor,
transportation, energy, education,
veterans affairs, health and human
services, and housing and urban
development; the attorney general;
the national security advisor; the
director of national intelligence;
and the Supreme Court justices.

Day 191

Lord, sometimes it's easier to give than to receive. I want to be a giver, to take the time to care for and help my friends when they need it. And help me learn to receive too—so that I'm not too proud to receive generosity from a friend.

Day 192

Lord, I give You my dreams.
I surrender my will to Yours.
When I am tempted to do
things my way, may I seek
Your guidance instead. When I try
to make things happen on my own,
give me mercy to see that Your
grace has everything covered.

Day 193

Lord, I want to be Your partner
in this life. I want to succeed in
all my endeavors, but I choose
to surrender to You first. I trust
that You will show me the way
to attain my goals by the work of
Your mighty and powerful hands.

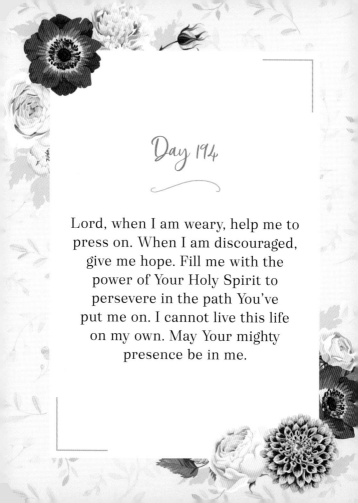

Day 194

Lord, when I am weary, help me to
press on. When I am discouraged,
give me hope. Fill me with the
power of Your Holy Spirit to
persevere in the path You've
put me on. I cannot live this life
on my own. May Your mighty
presence be in me.

Day 195

Lord, it can be so hard to forgive–
especially when I feel that other
people don't deserve it. But I don't
deserve Your forgiveness either,
and You freely forgive me when I
ask. Because of Your great mercy
toward me, help me to forgive
the people who've hurt me.

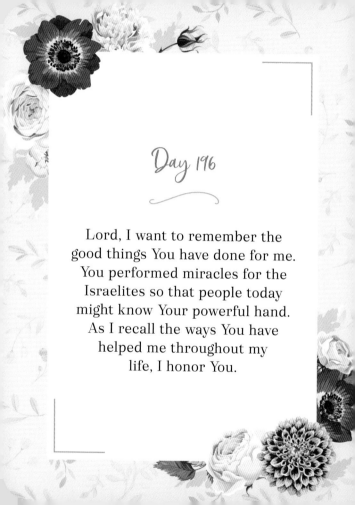

Day 196

Lord, I want to remember the good things You have done for me. You performed miracles for the Israelites so that people today might know Your powerful hand. As I recall the ways You have helped me throughout my life, I honor You.

Day 197

Lord, I thank You for our
missionaries, both foreign and
domestic. Empower them, fill them,
and sustain them as they seek
to fulfill Your great commission.
Give them godly wisdom and good
communication as they preach,
teach, disciple, and baptize
people from all nations.

Day 198

Lord, some of the things in my
past have led me far from You. I
want to come back and be in right
standing with You again. I ask for
forgiveness for the things I have
done wrong. Here I am, Lord.
I return to You.

Day 199

Lord, I prayed for this child, and
You have granted me what I asked.
Thank You for the miracle of this
new life. I pray Your blessing on
our precious baby. May our child
grow to be strong and healthy
in mind, soul, and spirit.

Day 200

Lord, help me forget the things
in my past that I need to leave
behind. Give me courage to press
on. There is a goal waiting for me,
a reward in heaven–and I want
to win the prize! Help me to
face forward and march
boldly into the future.

Day 201

Lord, heal me from oppression.
I pray for the shed blood of Jesus
over my life. Nothing can keep me
from You—neither death nor life,
neither angels nor demons,
neither the present nor the future,
nor any powers, neither height
nor depth, nor anything
else in all creation.

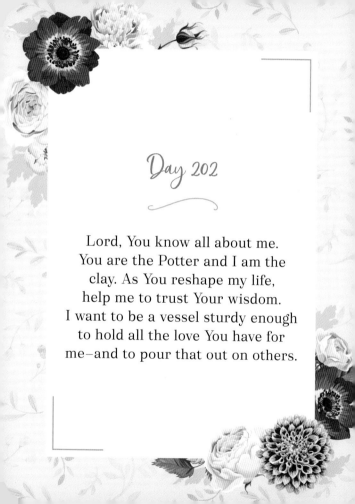

Day 202

Lord, You know all about me.
You are the Potter and I am the
clay. As You reshape my life,
help me to trust Your wisdom.
I want to be a vessel sturdy enough
to hold all the love You have for
me—and to pour that out on others.

Day 203

Lord, I'm free! For so long I was
bound in sin, selfishness, and
unhealthy ways of thinking.
I tried to change on my own,
but like a prisoner in handcuffs,
I was powerless. Praise You,
Lord–You loosed the chains
that held me.

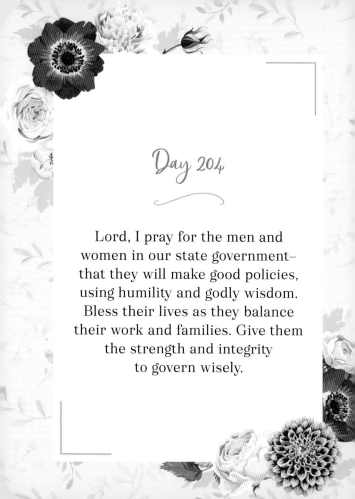

Day 204

Lord, I pray for the men and
women in our state government–
that they will make good policies,
using humility and godly wisdom.
Bless their lives as they balance
their work and families. Give them
the strength and integrity
to govern wisely.

Day 205

Lord, thank You for the bond
of friendship in our marriage.
I enjoy talking and sharing life
with my husband. Thank You for
our laughter and joy. Give us time
to reconnect on a playful level–in
sports, games, travel, or working
together around the house.

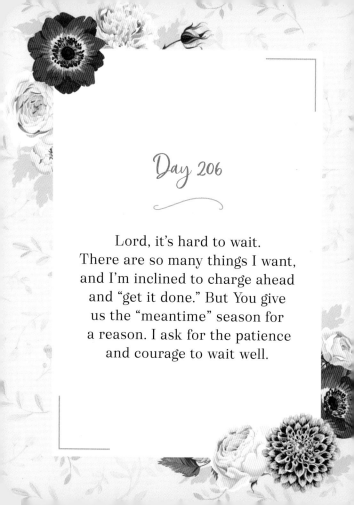

Day 206

Lord, it's hard to wait.
There are so many things I want,
and I'm inclined to charge ahead
and "get it done." But You give
us the "meantime" season for
a reason. I ask for the patience
and courage to wait well.

Day 207

Lord, I am tired of arguing about
money. Please give my husband
and me the ability to communicate
better in this area of our lives.
Help us to speak with integrity
and listen with respect
and understanding.

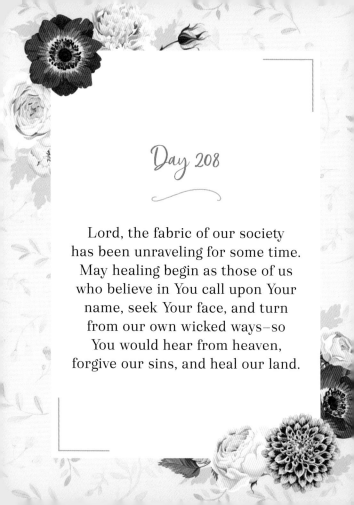

Day 208

Lord, the fabric of our society
has been unraveling for some time.
May healing begin as those of us
who believe in You call upon Your
name, seek Your face, and turn
from our own wicked ways–so
You would hear from heaven,
forgive our sins, and heal our land.

Day 209

Lord, I pray for the poor and needy.
Many need money, while others
are poor in spirit. Provide food and
water to meet their physical needs
and the Gospel of Jesus Christ and
His saving love to fill their souls.
Show me how I can be part
of the solution.

Day 210

Lord, I pray for each member of this church–that we would get along. Despite our variety of backgrounds and opinions, help us to live and worship in harmony. Give us the ability to value and respect our differences. Protect us against divisions, and help us to be like-minded.

Day 211

Lord, help me hold on to hope.
Abraham had great faith in You and
became the father of many nations.
Though he was old, You provided a
son for him and his wife, Sarah.
As You did for them, please fulfill
my longings–and Your vision
for my life's purpose.

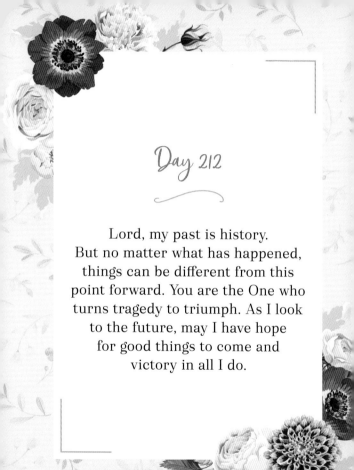

Day 212

Lord, my past is history.
But no matter what has happened,
things can be different from this
point forward. You are the One who
turns tragedy to triumph. As I look
to the future, may I have hope
for good things to come and
victory in all I do.

Day 213

Lord, I have prayed and healing hasn't come. It's hard to know why You do not heal when You clearly have the power to do so. Please help me not to focus on my present suffering, but to be transformed in my attitude.

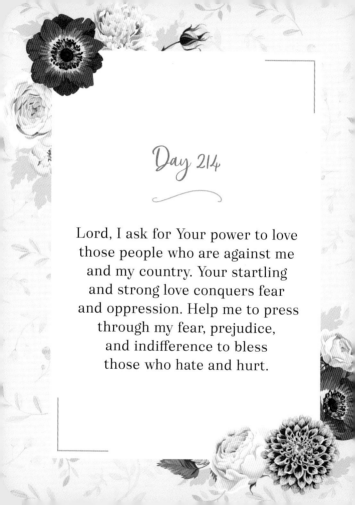

Day 214

Lord, I ask for Your power to love
those people who are against me
and my country. Your startling
and strong love conquers fear
and oppression. Help me to press
through my fear, prejudice,
and indifference to bless
those who hate and hurt.

Day 215

Lord, I pray that we would be a
welcoming church for members,
guests, and newcomers alike.
Help us to receive new people
with warmth and love. We were all
once "the new person," so help us
to be inclusive and make visitors
feel at home in our church.

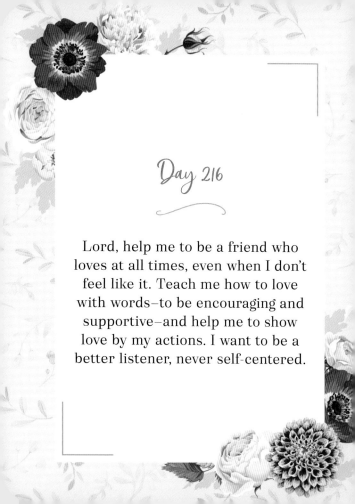

Day 216

Lord, help me to be a friend who loves at all times, even when I don't feel like it. Teach me how to love with words—to be encouraging and supportive—and help me to show love by my actions. I want to be a better listener, never self-centered.

Day 217

Lord, may our city leaders
lead with integrity, honesty,
and fairness. Help the people
I pray for now lead with justice,
grace, and mercy: the mayor,
our judges and court officials,
members of the police
and fire departments,
and other civic leaders.

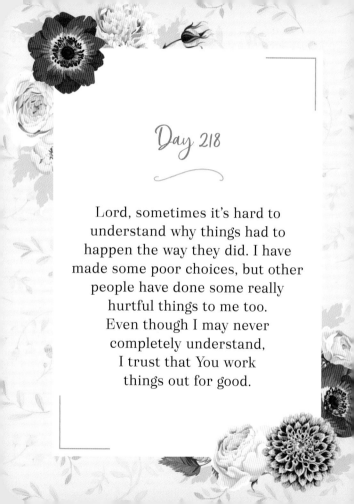

Day 218

Lord, sometimes it's hard to
understand why things had to
happen the way they did. I have
made some poor choices, but other
people have done some really
hurtful things to me too.
Even though I may never
completely understand,
I trust that You work
things out for good.

Day 219

Lord, it's hard to let go of things
that are comfortable and familiar,
even when they're not good for me
anymore. I need Your strong power
to release my grasp on the things
I cling to so tightly—like unhealthy
ways of thinking or relationships
that are not bearing fruit.

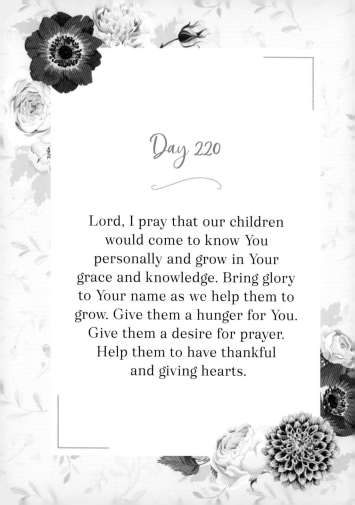

Day 220

Lord, I pray that our children
would come to know You
personally and grow in Your
grace and knowledge. Bring glory
to Your name as we help them to
grow. Give them a hunger for You.
Give them a desire for prayer.
Help them to have thankful
and giving hearts.

Day 221

Lord, thank You for the power to obey and follow Your ways. Your Word tells us that obedience leads to blessings. I ask for forgiveness when I have done wrong and for strength to make better choices. Help me to walk in faithfulness, empowered by Your Holy Spirit.

Day 222

Lord, Your love is so strong
that You swept down to snatch me
from the gravest times of my life.
You know how hard things have
been; I thought I was going to die.
But I didn't. And it's all because
of Your power of deliverance.
Praise You, Lord!

Day 223

Lord, I have neglected time with You. Please forgive me. Blow a fresh wind into the staleness of my life and revive my spirit. Help me put aside my selfishness and seek You first. Awaken my soul to the goodness of Your love, for You are my heart's desire.

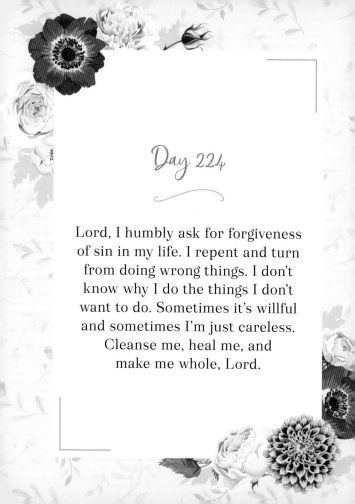

Day 224

Lord, I humbly ask for forgiveness
of sin in my life. I repent and turn
from doing wrong things. I don't
know why I do the things I don't
want to do. Sometimes it's willful
and sometimes I'm just careless.
Cleanse me, heal me, and
make me whole, Lord.

Day 225

Holy Spirit, I cannot live life on my own strength. I ask that You would come and fill me with Your presence. Empower me with discernment to make better life choices and energy to thrive–not just survive. Give me a heart to seek You and serve others.

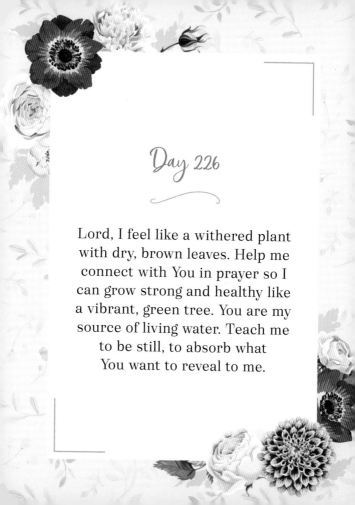

Day 226

Lord, I feel like a withered plant
with dry, brown leaves. Help me
connect with You in prayer so I
can grow strong and healthy like
a vibrant, green tree. You are my
source of living water. Teach me
to be still, to absorb what
You want to reveal to me.

Day 227

Lord, I want to live a life of love!
Show me what true love is–Your
love–so I can receive it and give it
away to others. Teach me to care
for my neighbor as I would care
for myself. Let love be my
motivation for action.

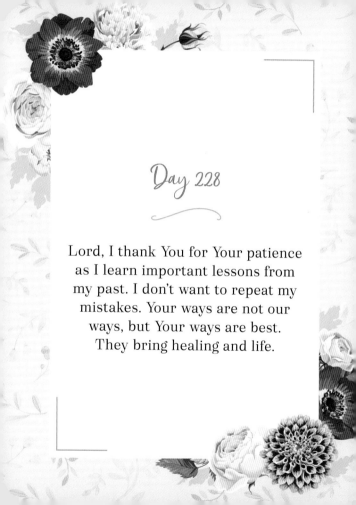

Day 228

Lord, I thank You for Your patience as I learn important lessons from my past. I don't want to repeat my mistakes. Your ways are not our ways, but Your ways are best. They bring healing and life.

Day 229

Lord, I have sought to find my significance in places other than Your heart. Forgive me for putting weight in what other people think or in my own efforts. Thank You that I have great worth no matter what I look like or do for a living.

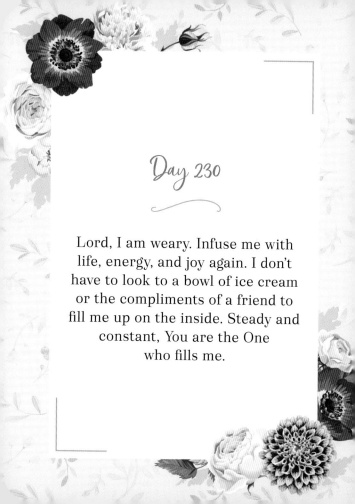

Day 230

Lord, I am weary. Infuse me with life, energy, and joy again. I don't have to look to a bowl of ice cream or the compliments of a friend to fill me up on the inside. Steady and constant, You are the One who fills me.

Day 231

Lord, I ask in Jesus' name that
You would bring Your light to the
dark places of Hollywood and
the entertainment industry.
Please raise up creative people
with good values to write and
produce entertainment that is
wholesome, nourishing,
and positive.

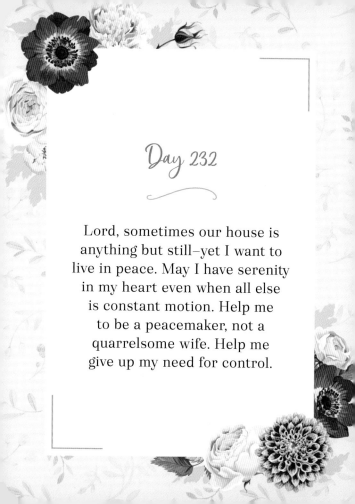

Day 232

Lord, sometimes our house is anything but still—yet I want to live in peace. May I have serenity in my heart even when all else is constant motion. Help me to be a peacemaker, not a quarrelsome wife. Help me give up my need for control.

Day 233

Lord, I humbly ask that You would forgive me for any ways I have hurt my friend. Help me to deal with things I'm aware of and bring to my mind the things I'm not. Please give me the courage and faith to forgive my friend when she hurts me.

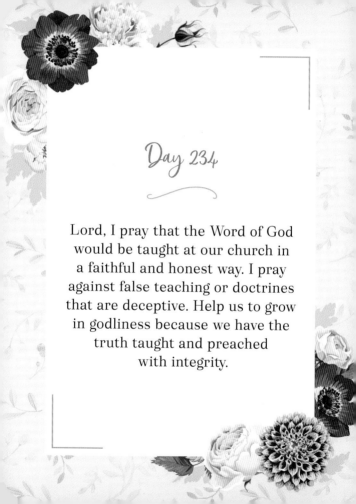

Day 234

Lord, I pray that the Word of God
would be taught at our church in
a faithful and honest way. I pray
against false teaching or doctrines
that are deceptive. Help us to grow
in godliness because we have the
truth taught and preached
with integrity.

Day 235

Lord, I need Your healing touch
on my past. I have lived too long
in ignorance, denial, and unbelief;
I thought nothing could ever
change. It seemed too late.
Now, Lord, please pour out
Your abundant grace on
me like a waterfall.
Shower me with healing.

Day 236

Lord, our world is so focused on outward appearances. But You're never like that. People may look at the hairstyles and the outfits, but You look at the heart. Please help me to work with what You've given me on the outside–as I also polish my inner character.

Day 237

Lord, I have been camping in
the past too long. Pull up my tent
stakes and help me to move on.
There is so much to live for today!
The past is over and the future
awaits. Today I choose to worship
You, my Lord and Maker.

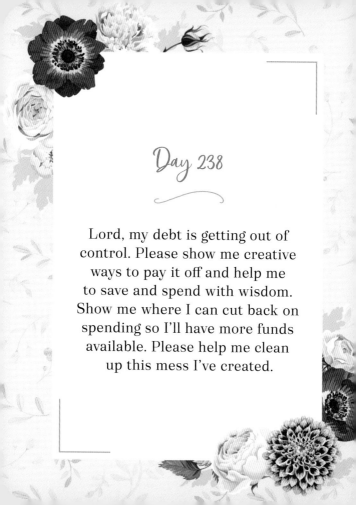

Day 238

Lord, my debt is getting out of
control. Please show me creative
ways to pay it off and help me
to save and spend with wisdom.
Show me where I can cut back on
spending so I'll have more funds
available. Please help me clean
up this mess I've created.

Day 239

Lord, I want to be a woman of wisdom, not foolishness. Help me to make right choices and conduct myself in a manner worthy of Your name. I pray that I would be honest and upright in my daily life so my actions reflect who You are.

Day 240

Lord, thank You for my church and the people who attend. Whether I know them all or not, help me to be a blessing to each person I meet. Help me to be an encourager, a listener. May we build each other up, not tear each other down.

Day 241

Lord, we need Your presence
in our schools and educational
system. I pray that the teachers
and administrators would lead with
kindness, patience, and strength as
they serve our children every day.
Help them to be knowledgeable
and prepared. Give them
energy and good hearts.

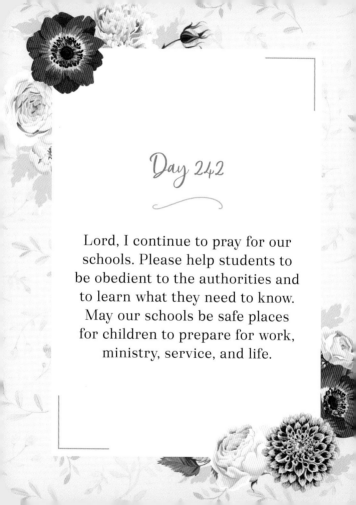

Day 242

Lord, I continue to pray for our schools. Please help students to be obedient to the authorities and to learn what they need to know. May our schools be safe places for children to prepare for work, ministry, service, and life.

Day 243

Lord, please create in me the fruit of self-control. Empower me to walk in Your Spirit's power and to flee temptation. Help me to change the channel or walk away from the food or put my credit cards out of reach when I've been using them too much.

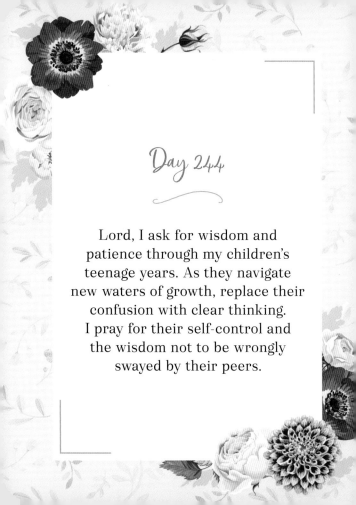

Day 244

Lord, I ask for wisdom and
patience through my children's
teenage years. As they navigate
new waters of growth, replace their
confusion with clear thinking.
I pray for their self-control and
the wisdom not to be wrongly
swayed by their peers.

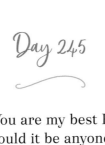

Day 245

Lord, You are my best Friend.
How could it be anyone else!
You are kind, loving, generous,
faithful, and giving. You always
listen, and You always care.
And You have the best advice.
But most of all, You laid down
Your life for me–for me, Lord!

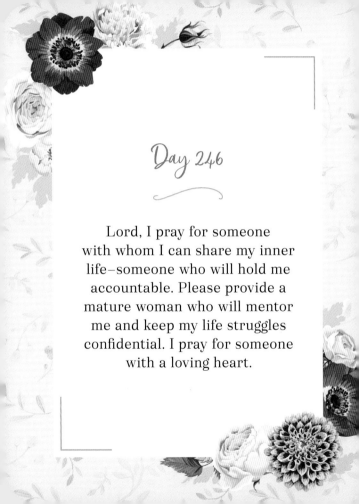

Day 246

Lord, I pray for someone
with whom I can share my inner
life—someone who will hold me
accountable. Please provide a
mature woman who will mentor
me and keep my life struggles
confidential. I pray for someone
with a loving heart.

Day 247

Lord, I continue to pray for a mentor, a person who won't judge me but will pray for and with me. Help me to be wise and responsible, but when I'm not, help me to learn and grow in my spiritual development. I want to be strong in Your strength.

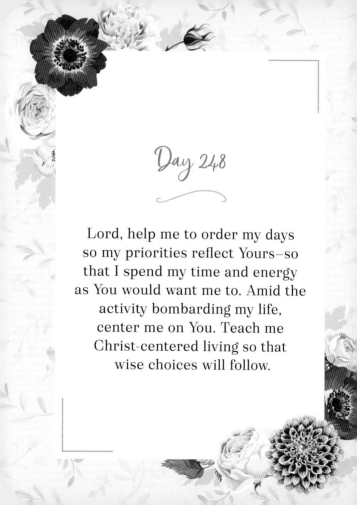

Day 248

Lord, help me to order my days
so my priorities reflect Yours—so
that I spend my time and energy
as You would want me to. Amid the
activity bombarding my life,
center me on You. Teach me
Christ-centered living so that
wise choices will follow.

Day 249

Lord, You are my God—and it is
my joy to give You my inner heart.
Cleanse me, fill me, heal me,
and help me to live with a joyful,
thankful heart. I want to be
a woman of prayer. I want to
make a difference in my world.

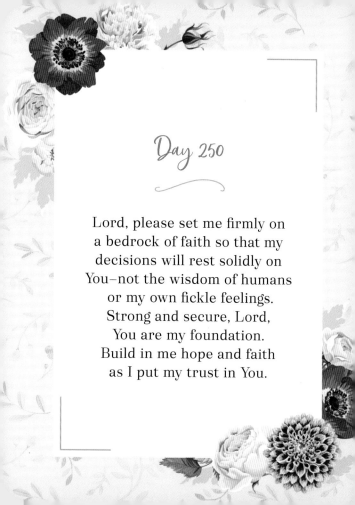

Day 250

Lord, please set me firmly on
a bedrock of faith so that my
decisions will rest solidly on
You—not the wisdom of humans
or my own fickle feelings.
Strong and secure, Lord,
You are my foundation.
Build in me hope and faith
as I put my trust in You.

Day 251

Lord, I thank You for my wonderful husband. I truly love him, but I need more; I need better communication with him. Help me not to fear asking for what I need emotionally. I pray that You would speak to his heart and that he would learn to listen.

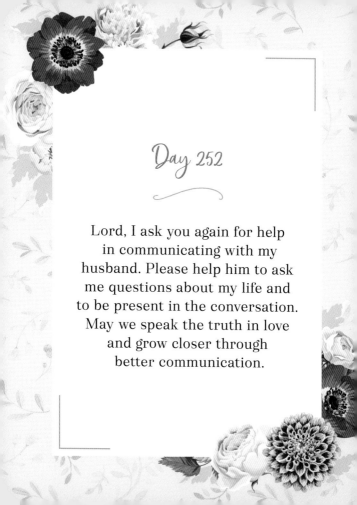

Day 252

Lord, I ask you again for help
in communicating with my
husband. Please help him to ask
me questions about my life and
to be present in the conversation.
May we speak the truth in love
and grow closer through
better communication.

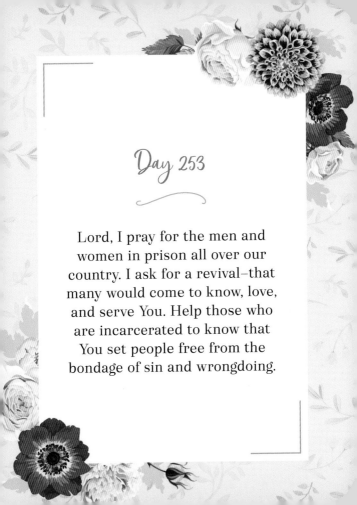

Day 253

Lord, I pray for the men and women in prison all over our country. I ask for a revival–that many would come to know, love, and serve You. Help those who are incarcerated to know that You set people free from the bondage of sin and wrongdoing.

Day 254

Lord, once again I bring before
You those who are in prison.
Help them to know that only You
offer a life of hope and peace.
In the darkness, help them to
find Christ's forgiveness, joy,
and light. Remind me to visit
those in prison and fulfill
Your commands.

Day 255

Lord, we want to worship You!
We praise Your holy name and
ask that You would bless us as
we worship You in spirit and in
truth. As we join together, let the
musicians, choir, and leaders guide
us in a chorus of resounding
praise and adoration.

Day 256

Lord, You have all power and
authority. You are the highest ruler
in the land—in the entire universe!
What a privilege it is to come
humbly yet boldly before You
and ask You to empower me
today. May Your blessings
flow through my life.

Day 257

In my life, Lord, there are many children besides my own. I pray for them today. I lift up my children's friends; my nieces, nephews, and other relatives; my neighborhood children; foster children I know; and church kids. I ask that You would bless them all through me.

Day 258

Lord, keep me from the foolishness of sin. I ask for wisdom and discernment to make wise choices. When I'm tempted, give me the strength to flee. When I'm uncertain, help me to know the right course of action. When I need good ideas, enlighten me with creativity and intelligence.

Day 259

Holy One, I revel in Your splendor.
I am amazed at all You are. Your
majesty, sovereignty, and glory are
a wonder to behold. That is why
I praise You. There is no one
like You, Lord. Let songs of
worship and praise be on
my tongue continually.

Day 260

Lord, I am praying for a person who is sick right now. She needs your healing touch on her body and her emotions. Heal her pain, Lord. Help her to sense Your presence, to know You are near. Be her comfort.

Day 261

Lord, I thank You for the families in our nation who are following You and generously serving those in need. I pray that You would build more families dedicated to upholding Your values. I ask for marriages to be strong and healthy.

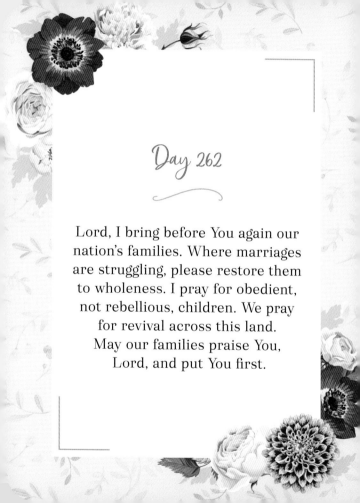

Day 262

Lord, I bring before You again our nation's families. Where marriages are struggling, please restore them to wholeness. I pray for obedient, not rebellious, children. We pray for revival across this land. May our families praise You, Lord, and put You first.

Day 263

Lord, I love to hike with You on this path of life. As we journey on, help me to do what is good—what You want me to do. The "good life" in Your eyes is for me to act justly, to love mercy, and to walk humbly before You.

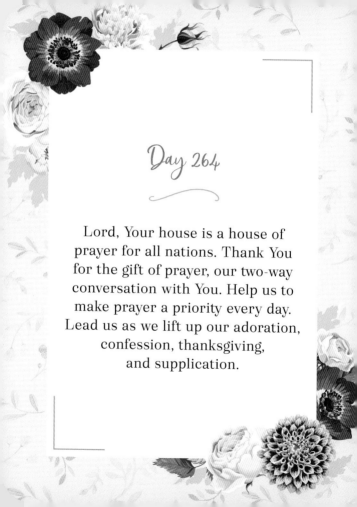

Day 264

Lord, Your house is a house of prayer for all nations. Thank You for the gift of prayer, our two-way conversation with You. Help us to make prayer a priority every day. Lead us as we lift up our adoration, confession, thanksgiving, and supplication.

Day 265

Lord, I feel as if my friends are distant and busy. They don't seem to have time for me. Maybe I've been preoccupied too. I ask that You would bring closer friendships into my life. I need to feel connected. I need their support and encouragement.

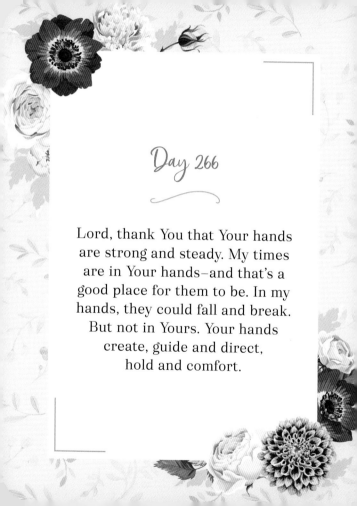

Day 266

Lord, thank You that Your hands
are strong and steady. My times
are in Your hands—and that's a
good place for them to be. In my
hands, they could fall and break.
But not in Yours. Your hands
create, guide and direct,
hold and comfort.

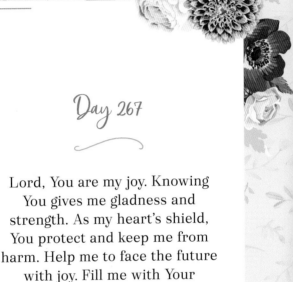

Day 267

Lord, You are my joy. Knowing You gives me gladness and strength. As my heart's shield, You protect and keep me from harm. Help me to face the future with joy. Fill me with Your good pleasures so I may bring enjoyment to my surroundings.

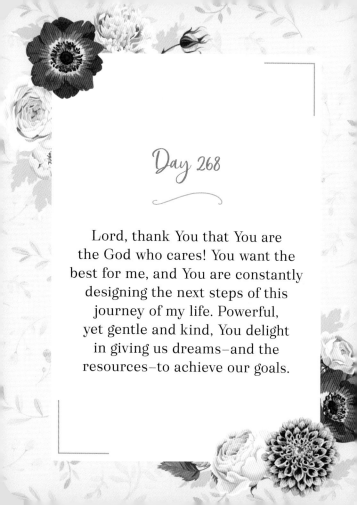

Day 268

Lord, thank You that You are
the God who cares! You want the
best for me, and You are constantly
designing the next steps of this
journey of my life. Powerful,
yet gentle and kind, You delight
in giving us dreams—and the
resources—to achieve our goals.

Day 269

Lord, I ask You to teach me how to make a difference in my workplace each day–even with a kind word or a smile to someone who needs it. Provide opportunities to share Your love; help me know just what to say when the time comes.

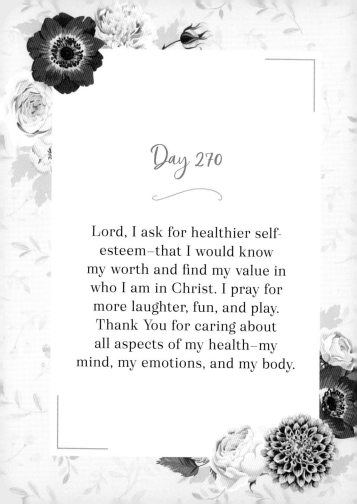

Day 270

Lord, I ask for healthier self-esteem—that I would know my worth and find my value in who I am in Christ. I pray for more laughter, fun, and play. Thank You for caring about all aspects of my health—my mind, my emotions, and my body.

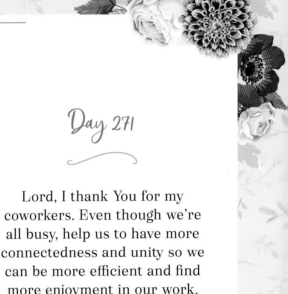

Day 271

Lord, I thank You for my coworkers. Even though we're all busy, help us to have more connectedness and unity so we can be more efficient and find more enjoyment in our work. Please bless me and my relationships in the workplace.

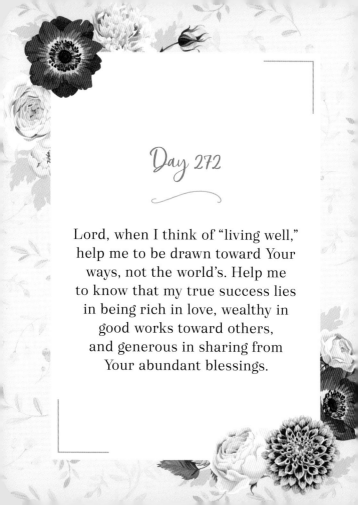

Day 272

Lord, when I think of "living well," help me to be drawn toward Your ways, not the world's. Help me to know that my true success lies in being rich in love, wealthy in good works toward others, and generous in sharing from Your abundant blessings.

Day 273

Lord, I need a new friend. It's hard
to find someone who cares and
makes the time for a new person
in her life. As I seek to extend
the hand of friendship to others,
give me wisdom to know
which relationships to pursue.
Bless me with good friends.

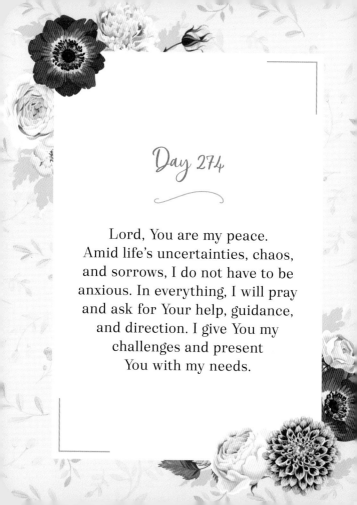

Day 274

Lord, You are my peace.
Amid life's uncertainties, chaos,
and sorrows, I do not have to be
anxious. In everything, I will pray
and ask for Your help, guidance,
and direction. I give You my
challenges and present
You with my needs.

Day 275

Lord, I am looking forward to my
future with You—both here on earth
and later in heaven. One day I will
be changed in a moment, in the
twinkling of an eye—and we will
be together forever. I can't even
imagine how beautiful and
glorious that will be!

Day 276

Lord, we need a revival in our
marriage. Please restore the
connection in our emotions
and intimacy. Daily living tires us,
and we need time together for true
closeness, not just familiarity.
I pray that we can rediscover the
joy of our love for each other.

Day 277

Lord, as I share with others the
amazing things You have done
in my life, help me to be a good
listener too. Through Your Spirit
may I show I care about my friends.
Give me wisdom to know when
my ears should be open
and my mouth shut.

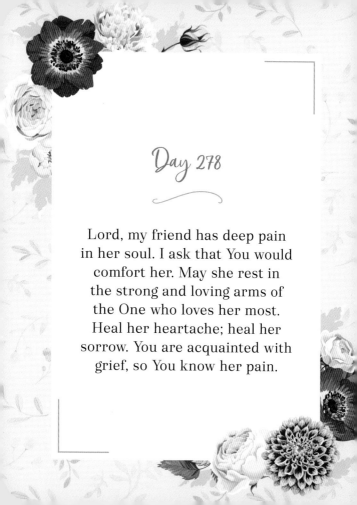

Day 278

Lord, my friend has deep pain
in her soul. I ask that You would
comfort her. May she rest in
the strong and loving arms of
the One who loves her most.
Heal her heartache; heal her
sorrow. You are acquainted with
grief, so You know her pain.

Day 279

Lord, I need wisdom in dealing with my adversaries. Teach me Your ways of justice, and help me to do what is right. I will not repay anyone evil for evil. I will not take it into my own hands, but I will allow You to avenge.

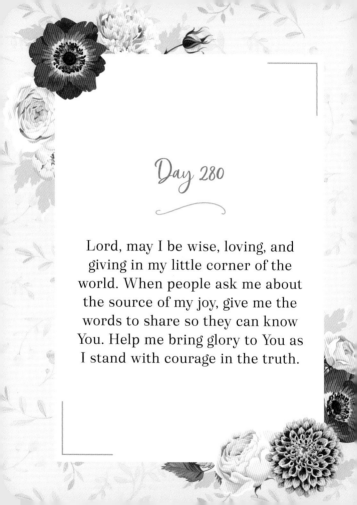

Day 280

Lord, may I be wise, loving, and giving in my little corner of the world. When people ask me about the source of my joy, give me the words to share so they can know You. Help me bring glory to You as I stand with courage in the truth.

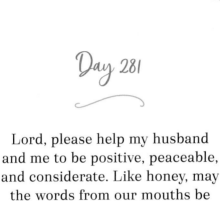

Day 281

Lord, please help my husband
and me to be positive, peaceable,
and considerate. Like honey, may
the words from our mouths be
sweet to the soul and healing to
the bones. Help us both to be
better listeners and to seek
to understand each other.

Day 282

Lord, I am glad to know that You have plans for me—because the future is so unclear in my mind. You desire to prosper me, not to harm. As the Giver of all good gifts, You wrap up hope and a future as my present.

Day 283

Lord, help us to discover and use
our spiritual gifts, those talents and
abilities You've given us to serve
You in the church and in outreach
ministries. We are many, but we
form one body. We have different
gifts, according to what You've
graciously given, but we
serve each other.

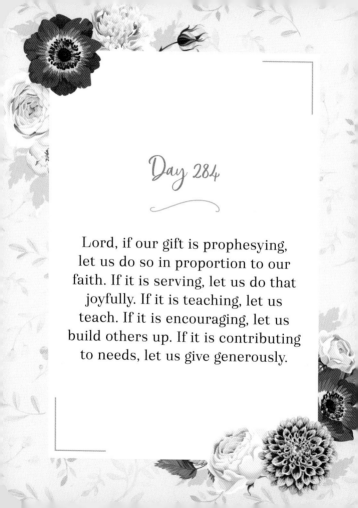

Day 284

Lord, if our gift is prophesying,
let us do so in proportion to our
faith. If it is serving, let us do that
joyfully. If it is teaching, let us
teach. If it is encouraging, let us
build others up. If it is contributing
to needs, let us give generously.

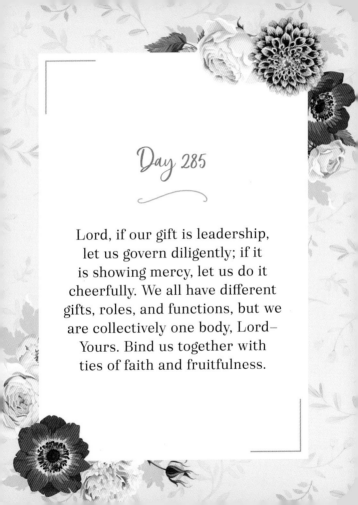

Day 285

Lord, if our gift is leadership,
let us govern diligently; if it
is showing mercy, let us do it
cheerfully. We all have different
gifts, roles, and functions, but we
are collectively one body, Lord—
Yours. Bind us together with
ties of faith and fruitfulness.

Day 286

Lord, sometimes my circumstances can be overwhelming. I don't want to be robbed of happiness and emotional stability. Please keep me in perfect peace as I focus my eyes on You rather than my problems. Let my mind be steady. Let my heart trust that You will see me through.

Day 287

Lord, please help my husband
and me to make our words kind,
not harsh, as we seek to prioritize
and find order in our finances.
Even when we don't agree, help us
to see the other person's point
of view and find ways to
resolve our conflicts.

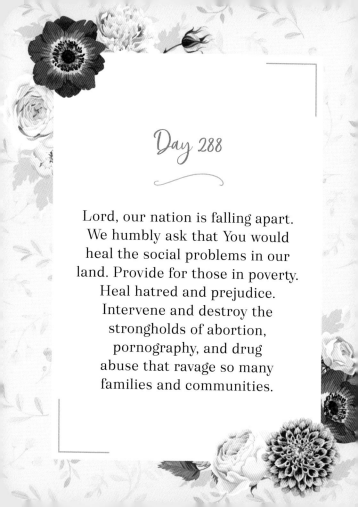

Day 288

Lord, our nation is falling apart.
We humbly ask that You would
heal the social problems in our
land. Provide for those in poverty.
Heal hatred and prejudice.
Intervene and destroy the
strongholds of abortion,
pornography, and drug
abuse that ravage so many
families and communities.

Day 289

Lord, I don't want peace to be
a once-in-a-while thing–I want
to know peace as a way of life.
Make me a conduit that brings
harmony to all my relationships.
Even when life is busy, I want to
be a person who takes time
to listen to others.

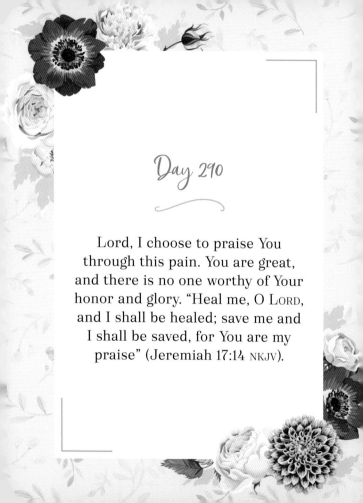

Day 290

Lord, I choose to praise You through this pain. You are great, and there is no one worthy of Your honor and glory. "Heal me, O Lord, and I shall be healed; save me and I shall be saved, for You are my praise" (Jeremiah 17:14 NKJV).

Day 291

May all the people I pray for now
be faithful stewards of their offices
and serve the people of our state
for the glory of God's name:
our state representatives and
senators, our governor, and our
state Supreme Court justices.

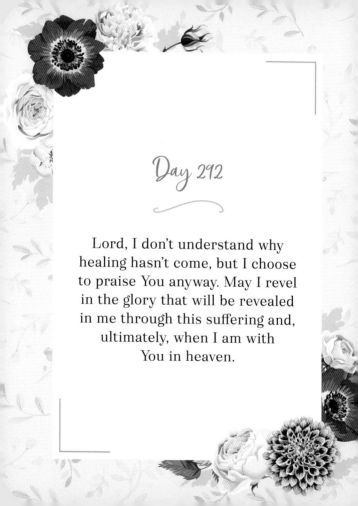

Day 292

Lord, I don't understand why
healing hasn't come, but I choose
to praise You anyway. May I revel
in the glory that will be revealed
in me through this suffering and,
ultimately, when I am with
You in heaven.

Day 213

Lord, I pray against the negative
messages coming out of the
entertainment industry–the
intense violence and sexuality
portrayed on the internet and
television, and in movies, books,
music, magazines, and other media.
Open the way for a bright new day
in our nation's entertainment
and media choices.

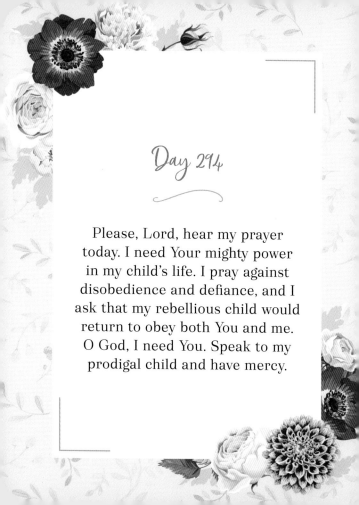

Day 294

Please, Lord, hear my prayer today. I need Your mighty power in my child's life. I pray against disobedience and defiance, and I ask that my rebellious child would return to obey both You and me. O God, I need You. Speak to my prodigal child and have mercy.

Day 295

Lord, thank You that Your great love conquers fear! I can love people freely because You live in me. I may be accepted or not, but either way I can love with confidence because Your perfect love drives out fear. Give me the courage to live that life of love.

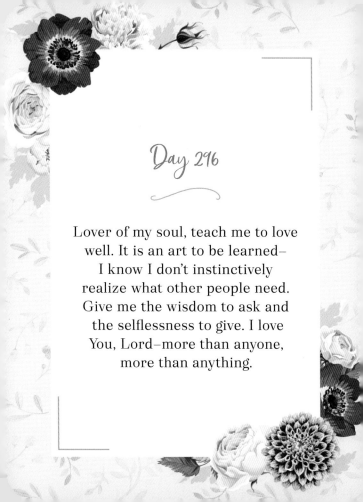

Day 296

Lover of my soul, teach me to love
well. It is an art to be learned–
I know I don't instinctively
realize what other people need.
Give me the wisdom to ask and
the selflessness to give. I love
You, Lord–more than anyone,
more than anything.

Day 297

Lord, I ask for Your insight as I teach my children about the wise use of money. Help me to impress upon them the importance of saving, tithing, and giving as well as spending in balanced ways.

Day 298

Lord, I have been so lonely lately–I need more friends. In Your graciousness, please provide for my need for companionship. But You are the Giver of good things, and I trust that You will bring the right people at the right time.

Day 299

Lord, I want to be a blessing to my extended family. I will pray for the ones You bring to mind. Help me to be sincere in honoring them. I pray for their needs, their salvation, and their healing. May they also learn to know and enjoy You.

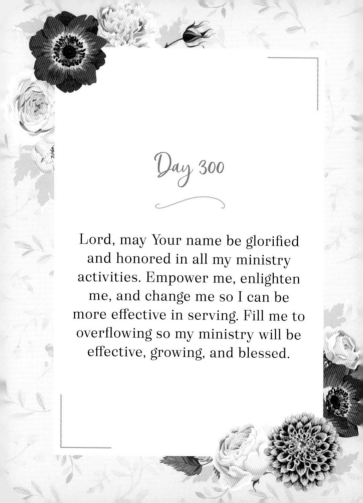

Day 300

Lord, may Your name be glorified
and honored in all my ministry
activities. Empower me, enlighten
me, and change me so I can be
more effective in serving. Fill me to
overflowing so my ministry will be
effective, growing, and blessed.

Day 301

Lord, I give You this discomfort,
and I ask in the name and power of
Jesus that You would take it away.
Help me and heal me completely
from my hurt. Let my heart ache
only for the comfort and healing
balm of Your presence.

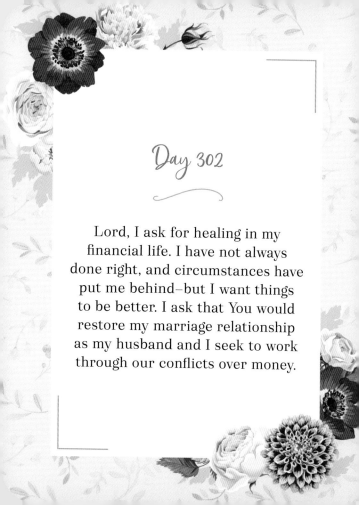

Day 302

Lord, I ask for healing in my financial life. I have not always done right, and circumstances have put me behind—but I want things to be better. I ask that You would restore my marriage relationship as my husband and I seek to work through our conflicts over money.

Day 303

Lord, I'm tired–and sometimes
I want to give up. Life is not easy.
In the midst of the trials, Lord,
help me never to give up hope
that You'll come through for me.
Help me to trust Your ways and
Your impeccable timing.

Day 304

Lord, I thank You for the faithful servants who teach in our Sunday school, Bible studies, and small groups. Though we all have different functions in the church, we are all one body— and I thank You that You knit us all together in unity.

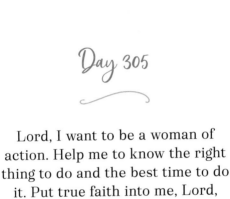

Day 305

Lord, I want to be a woman of
action. Help me to know the right
thing to do and the best time to do
it. Put true faith into me, Lord,
so I can perform the good works
You have for me to accomplish.

Day 306

Lord, help me to have more confidence–not in myself but in You. I don't want to be proud or conceited, but I don't want to be a doormat either. Give me a teachable heart. You have so much to show me, and I want to learn Your ways.

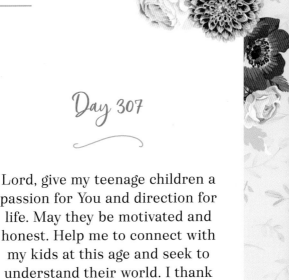

Day 307

Lord, give my teenage children a passion for You and direction for life. May they be motivated and honest. Help me to connect with my kids at this age and seek to understand their world. I thank You that the battle is not mine to fight but Yours, Lord.

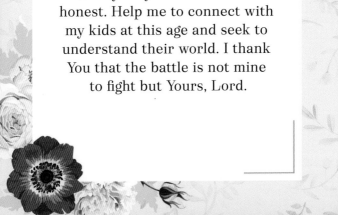

Day 308

Lord, Your Word says that we are not to think of ourselves more highly than we ought but to think of ourselves with sober judgment, in accordance with the faith You have given us. Help me not to have pride, arrogance, or conceit in my heart.

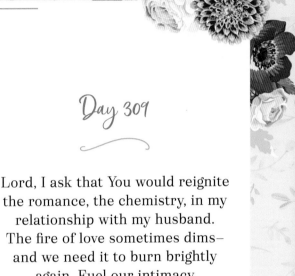

Day 309

Lord, I ask that You would reignite the romance, the chemistry, in my relationship with my husband. The fire of love sometimes dims– and we need it to burn brightly again. Fuel our intimacy with restored affection and passion for each other.

Day 310

Revive us, O Lord! I pray for
a great awakening of hope,
healing, and salvation in America.
Forgive us our personal sins and
the sins of our people. May our
nation fulfill her great destiny
and purposes. Awaken us
to our need for You and our
total dependence on You.

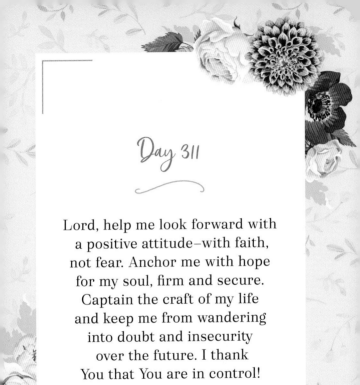

Day 311

Lord, help me look forward with
a positive attitude–with faith,
not fear. Anchor me with hope
for my soul, firm and secure.
Captain the craft of my life
and keep me from wandering
into doubt and insecurity
over the future. I thank
You that You are in control!

Day 312

Lord, I thank You for providing for my needs. I give You my worries and fears–those nagging thoughts about lacking money for clothes, food, and the basics of life. You feed the sparrows in the field, Lord–You'll certainly help me and my family.

Day 313

Lord, would You please show me how I can reach out to someone who needs a friend? Bring to mind people with whom I can share the love of Christ. Let my words and actions reflect Your love, acceptance, and compassion.

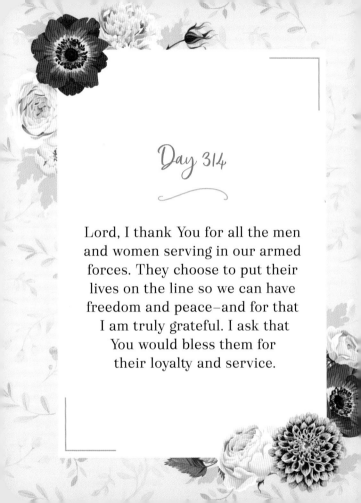

Day 314

Lord, I thank You for all the men and women serving in our armed forces. They choose to put their lives on the line so we can have freedom and peace—and for that I am truly grateful. I ask that You would bless them for their loyalty and service.

Day 315

Lord, I lift up to You again
those serving in our military.
Protect them and keep them
safe. Comfort them and give them
strength when they are away
from loved ones. Bless too,
the families who send soldiers
to war or for duty overseas.
Please meet their every need.

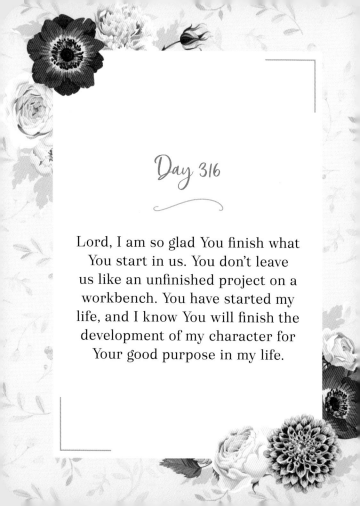

Day 316

Lord, I am so glad You finish what You start in us. You don't leave us like an unfinished project on a workbench. You have started my life, and I know You will finish the development of my character for Your good purpose in my life.

Day 317

Lord, I thank You that the Bible helps me to be "wise for salvation through faith. . .in Christ Jesus" (2 Timothy 3:15 NKJV). Your Word comforts me and gives me strength when I need it. Fill me with Your words of life and hope so I may use them to encourage others.

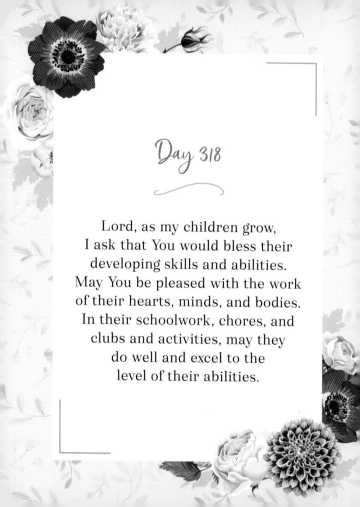

Day 318

Lord, as my children grow,
I ask that You would bless their
developing skills and abilities.
May You be pleased with the work
of their hearts, minds, and bodies.
In their schoolwork, chores, and
clubs and activities, may they
do well and excel to the
level of their abilities.

Day 319

Lord, You know my friend's needs.
But sometimes I don't know what
to say or how to pray. Holy Spirit,
You are the One who helps us in
our weakness. When I don't know
what to pray for, You intercede
for me with groans that
words cannot express.

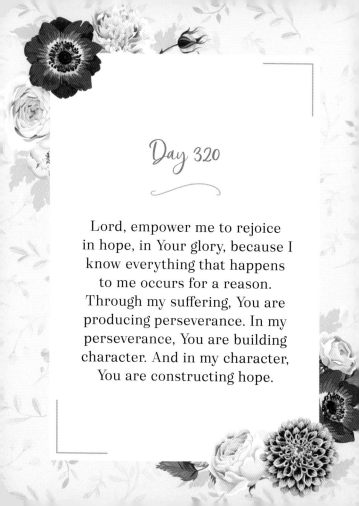

Day 320

Lord, empower me to rejoice
in hope, in Your glory, because I
know everything that happens
to me occurs for a reason.
Through my suffering, You are
producing perseverance. In my
perseverance, You are building
character. And in my character,
You are constructing hope.

Day 321

Lord, I look to the Bible for truth
and freedom so I can live, with love
and victory, the abundant life
You promise to all who believe.
Help me to know You better. . .
to be a doer of the Word, not just
a hearer. . .to live what I believe.

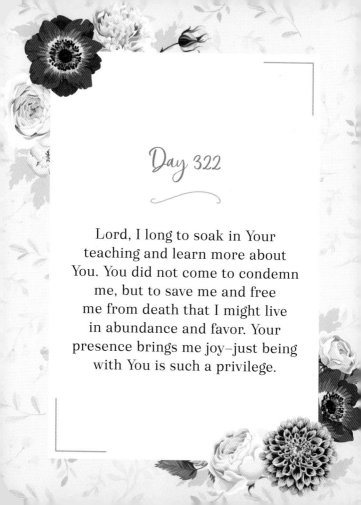

Day 322

Lord, I long to soak in Your
teaching and learn more about
You. You did not come to condemn
me, but to save me and free
me from death that I might live
in abundance and favor. Your
presence brings me joy–just being
with You is such a privilege.

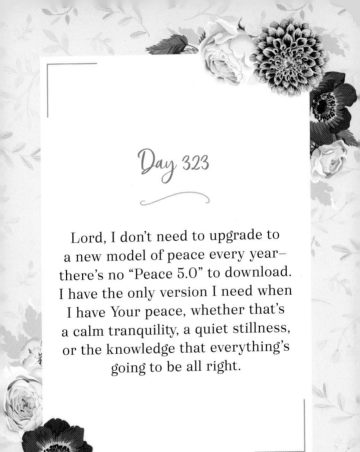

Day 323

Lord, I don't need to upgrade to
a new model of peace every year—
there's no "Peace 5.0" to download.
I have the only version I need when
I have Your peace, whether that's
a calm tranquility, a quiet stillness,
or the knowledge that everything's
going to be all right.

Day 324

Lord, You have blessed me with a
wonderful husband. He is truly my
best friend. Help us to keep our
attitude positive, to smile and have
fun together. Keep us connected
in love and friendship; help us
to truly enjoy each other.

Day 325

Lord, please help me to give my
children what they need–whether
it's a hug or a pat on the back,
kind words or extra encouragement
on a hard homework assignment.
May I learn from You how to bring
out the best in each of them.

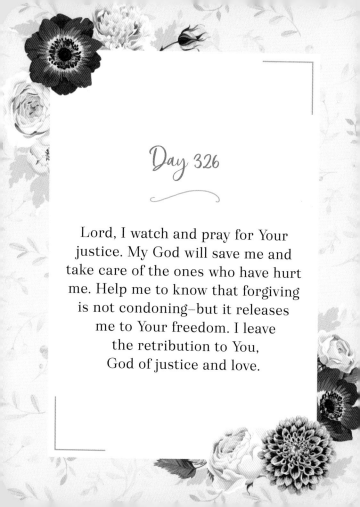

Day 326

Lord, I watch and pray for Your
justice. My God will save me and
take care of the ones who have hurt
me. Help me to know that forgiving
is not condoning—but it releases
me to Your freedom. I leave
the retribution to You,
God of justice and love.

Day 327

Lord, from the nursery at church to the orphanages across the sea, there are children who need love. From the streets of Columbus to the slums of Calcutta, people need to hear the Gospel. Show me where I can give and serve. Use my abilities and finances to help.

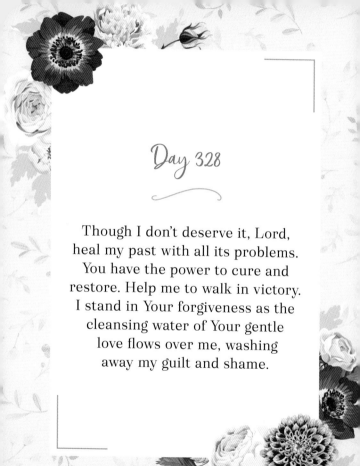

Day 328

Though I don't deserve it, Lord,
heal my past with all its problems.
You have the power to cure and
restore. Help me to walk in victory.
I stand in Your forgiveness as the
cleansing water of Your gentle
love flows over me, washing
away my guilt and shame.

Day 329

Lord, for all You are and all You do, I am grateful. I give You praise for the blessings in my life. You are worthy and wonderful. Thank You for Your loving-kindness and mercy that cleanse my soul and let me be in right standing with You.

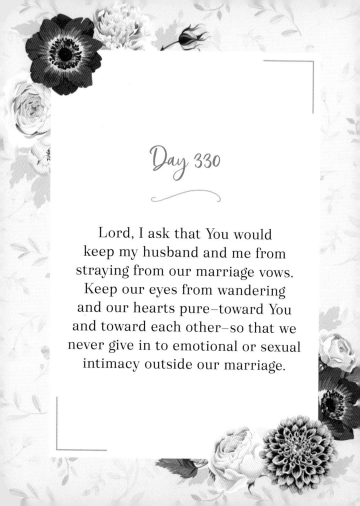

Day 330

Lord, I ask that You would
keep my husband and me from
straying from our marriage vows.
Keep our eyes from wandering
and our hearts pure—toward You
and toward each other—so that we
never give in to emotional or sexual
intimacy outside our marriage.

Day 331

Lord, thank You for Your healing balm that covers the hurt I've experienced in this friendship. Your grace covers me. Your love repairs my brokenness, and You give me the ability to love again. Help me to put aside the wounds of my heart and be a friend again.

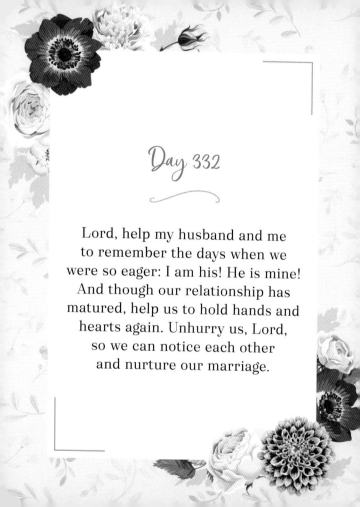

Day 332

Lord, help my husband and me
to remember the days when we
were so eager: I am his! He is mine!
And though our relationship has
matured, help us to hold hands and
hearts again. Unhurry us, Lord,
so we can notice each other
and nurture our marriage.

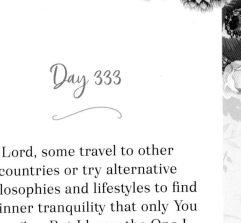

Day 333

Lord, some travel to other countries or try alternative philosophies and lifestyles to find an inner tranquility that only You can give. But I know the One I believe; I have a strong conviction that He is willing and able to help me. Thank You for Your peace!

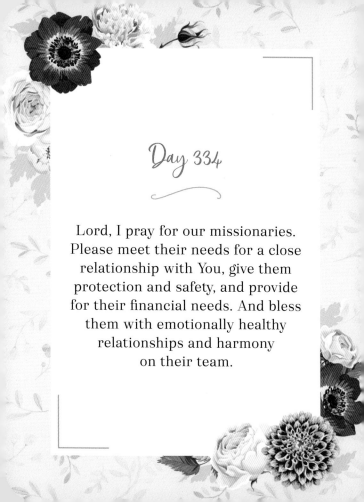

Day 334

Lord, I pray for our missionaries.
Please meet their needs for a close
relationship with You, give them
protection and safety, and provide
for their financial needs. And bless
them with emotionally healthy
relationships and harmony
on their team.

Day 335

Lord, I pray for restoration as Your gracious love revives my child's heart. Bring my child back to You and to our family again. Give him/her ears to hear, eyes to see, and a heart to receive Your love gift of salvation. Draw my child to Yourself, I pray.

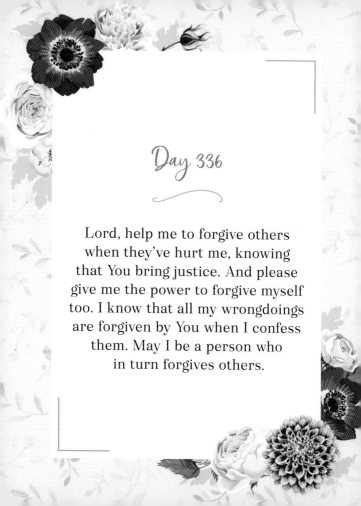

Day 336

Lord, help me to forgive others
when they've hurt me, knowing
that You bring justice. And please
give me the power to forgive myself
too. I know that all my wrongdoings
are forgiven by You when I confess
them. May I be a person who
in turn forgives others.

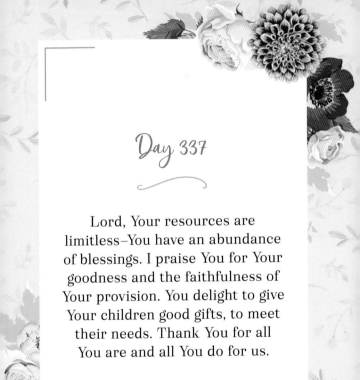

Day 337

Lord, Your resources are
limitless—You have an abundance
of blessings. I praise You for Your
goodness and the faithfulness of
Your provision. You delight to give
Your children good gifts, to meet
their needs. Thank You for all
You are and all You do for us.

Day 338

Lord, You care, You comfort,
and You really listen. Here,
in Your presence, I am loved,
I am renewed, and I am very happy.
You are awesome, and I delight
to know You and tell others
about You. I will praise You,
O Lord, with all my heart.

Day 339

Lord, I have so much to do—please help me! Deadlines and details swirl around me like a swarm of bees. I feel intense pressure with my heavy workload. Help me to do what needs to be done each day so I can stop worrying and rest well at night.

Day 340

Lord, as I look out for the needs
of others, I pray that I would be
a vessel of Your blessing and joy.
Give me eyes to see the needs
and a heart to respond. Help me
to serve others with the right
motives. Let me lead with love.

Day 341

Lord, thank You that I can have a
calm spirit–because You are the
Prince of Peace. Your name, Jesus,
has the authority to make fear and
worry flee. Your name has power!
Keep me safe and protected.
Cover me and be near me.

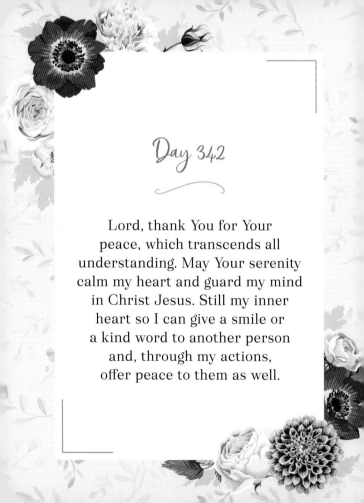

Day 342

Lord, thank You for Your
peace, which transcends all
understanding. May Your serenity
calm my heart and guard my mind
in Christ Jesus. Still my inner
heart so I can give a smile or
a kind word to another person
and, through my actions,
offer peace to them as well.

Day 343

Lord, at times I'm so affected by this world–I am tempted to want what others have or long for things I see on television. Change my attitude, Lord. Help me to understand that acquiring more "stuff" won't necessarily make me happy. Being filled with You brings true contentment.

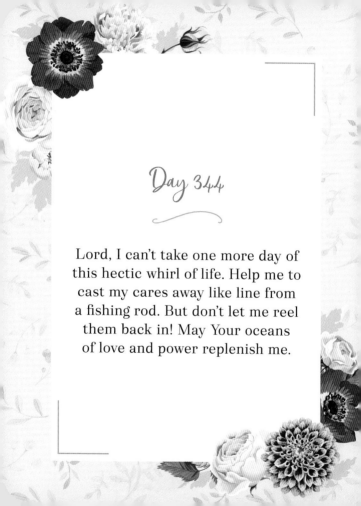

Day 344

Lord, I can't take one more day of
this hectic whirl of life. Help me to
cast my cares away like line from
a fishing rod. But don't let me reel
them back in! May Your oceans
of love and power replenish me.

Day 345

Lord, I give You my anxiety
and stress–I release it all to You.
As Your peace covers me, the peace
that passes all understanding,
may it guard my heart and mind
in Christ Jesus. I rest in the
comfort of Your love.

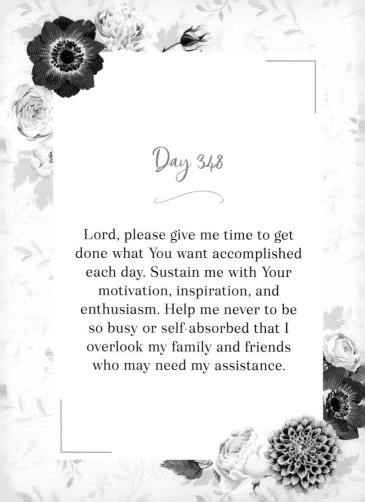

Day 348

Lord, please give me time to get done what You want accomplished each day. Sustain me with Your motivation, inspiration, and enthusiasm. Help me never to be so busy or self-absorbed that I overlook my family and friends who may need my assistance.

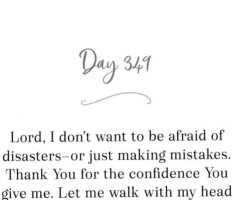

Day 349

Lord, I don't want to be afraid of
disasters—or just making mistakes.
Thank You for the confidence You
give me. Let me walk with my head
high because I know who I am
in Christ: I am Yours!

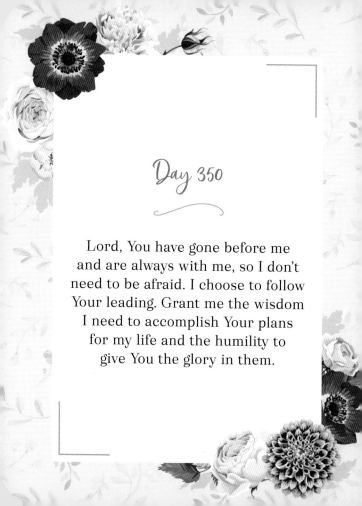

Day 350

Lord, You have gone before me
and are always with me, so I don't
need to be afraid. I choose to follow
Your leading. Grant me the wisdom
I need to accomplish Your plans
for my life and the humility to
give You the glory in them.

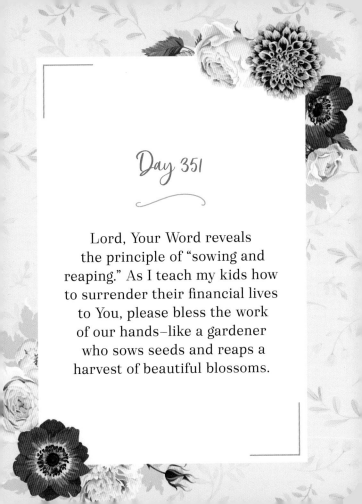

Day 351

Lord, Your Word reveals
the principle of "sowing and
reaping." As I teach my kids how
to surrender their financial lives
to You, please bless the work
of our hands—like a gardener
who sows seeds and reaps a
harvest of beautiful blossoms.

Day 352

Lord, I humbly ask You to make me well. And if You choose not to, Lord, help me to praise You anyway, looking for the good purpose You have in my life. Your will be done, Father.

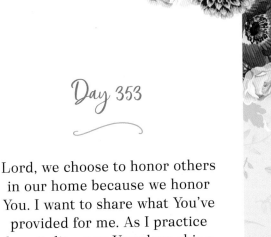

Day 353

Lord, we choose to honor others in our home because we honor You. I want to share what You've provided for me. As I practice hospitality, may Your love shine through my life. Help me to have a welcoming heart.

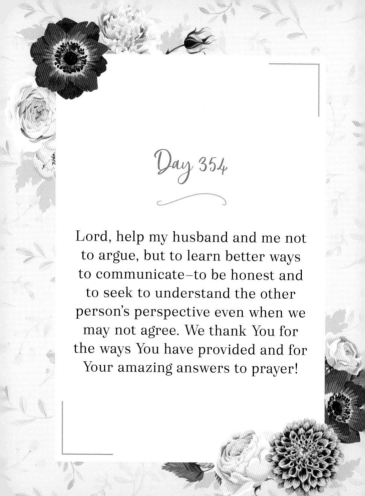

Day 354

Lord, help my husband and me not to argue, but to learn better ways to communicate—to be honest and to seek to understand the other person's perspective even when we may not agree. We thank You for the ways You have provided and for Your amazing answers to prayer!

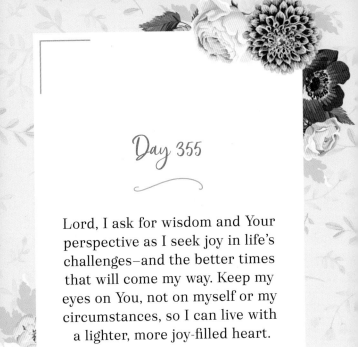

Day 355

Lord, I ask for wisdom and Your perspective as I seek joy in life's challenges—and the better times that will come my way. Keep my eyes on You, not on myself or my circumstances, so I can live with a lighter, more joy-filled heart.

Day 356

Lord, I pray for more discernment, so that in whatever comes my way, I will have the grace to think, speak, and act with a good and godly attitude. Help me to act with integrity, so I become a person who keeps her promises and commitments.

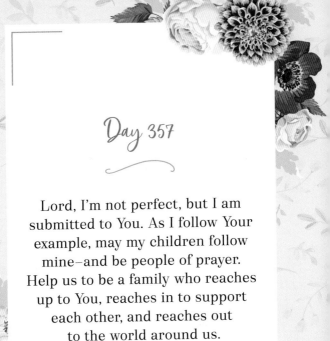

Day 357

Lord, I'm not perfect, but I am submitted to You. As I follow Your example, may my children follow mine—and be people of prayer. Help us to be a family who reaches up to You, reaches in to support each other, and reaches out to the world around us.

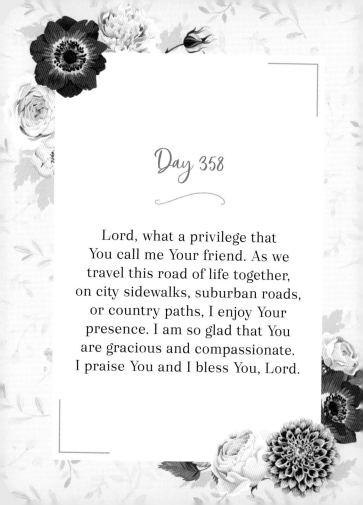

Day 358

Lord, what a privilege that
You call me Your friend. As we
travel this road of life together,
on city sidewalks, suburban roads,
or country paths, I enjoy Your
presence. I am so glad that You
are gracious and compassionate.
I praise You and I bless You, Lord.

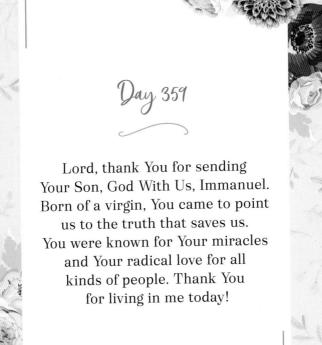

Day 359

Lord, thank You for sending
Your Son, God With Us, Immanuel.
Born of a virgin, You came to point
us to the truth that saves us.
You were known for Your miracles
and Your radical love for all
kinds of people. Thank You
for living in me today!

Day 360

Lord, teach me about surrender,
knowing You lift me up to do Your
good purposes. Transform me.
Teach me to follow You. I don't
know where I would be without
You. Help me to remain faithful
in prayer, Lord, and fully
committed to You.

Day 361

My ultimate trust is in You, Lord, not in any person. As I report to You each day for guidance, help me to serve You well. Turn to me and let Your love and mercy shine on me so I can be a light to others.

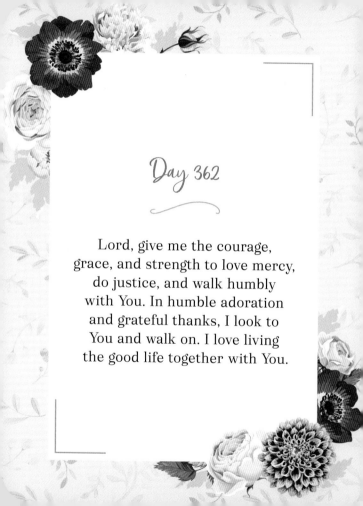

Day 362

Lord, give me the courage,
grace, and strength to love mercy,
do justice, and walk humbly
with You. In humble adoration
and grateful thanks, I look to
You and walk on. I love living
the good life together with You.

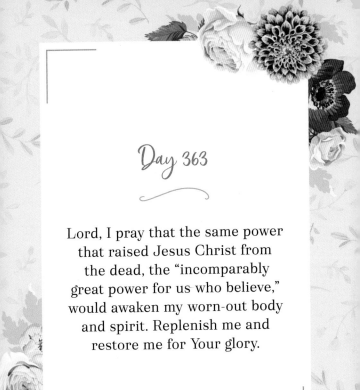

Day 363

Lord, I pray that the same power that raised Jesus Christ from the dead, the "incomparably great power for us who believe," would awaken my worn-out body and spirit. Replenish me and restore me for Your glory.

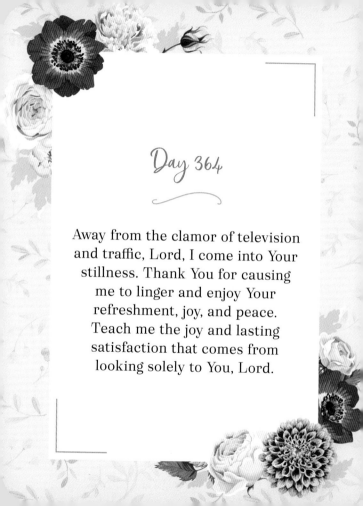

Day 364

Away from the clamor of television and traffic, Lord, I come into Your stillness. Thank You for causing me to linger and enjoy Your refreshment, joy, and peace. Teach me the joy and lasting satisfaction that comes from looking solely to You, Lord.

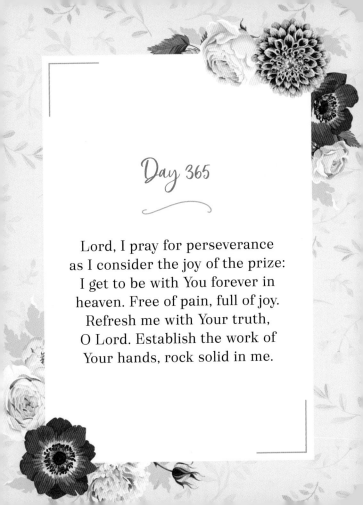

Day 365

Lord, I pray for perseverance
as I consider the joy of the prize:
I get to be with You forever in
heaven. Free of pain, full of joy.
Refresh me with Your truth,
O Lord. Establish the work of
Your hands, rock solid in me.

Read Thru the Bible in a Year Plan

Strengthen Your Faith by
Growing Your Prayer Life

The Prayer Map for Women

This engaging prayer journal is a fun and creative way for you to more fully experience the power of prayer in your life. Each page guides you to write out specific thoughts, ideas, and lists. . .which then creates a specific "map" for you to follow as you talk to God.

Spiral Bound / 978-1-68322-557-7 / $7.99

The Prayer Map for a Less Stressed Life

This engaging prayer journal is a fun and creative way for you to more fully experience the power of prayer in your busy life. Each page guides you to write out specific thoughts, ideas, and lists. . . which then creates a specific "map" for you to follow as you talk to God.

Spiral Bound / 978-1-64352-716-1 / $7.99